Child Development

Child Development

Second Edition

Geoffrey Brown

Open Books

First published in 1977 by Open Books Publishing Ltd
Beaumont House, Wells, Somerset BA5 2LD, England

5th printing 1983
Second Edition revised and reset 1986

© Geoffrey Brown 1986

ISBN: 0 7291 0179 7

Typeset by V & M Graphics Ltd, Aylesbury, Bucks
Printed and bound in Great Britain by A. Wheaton & Co Ltd, Exeter

Contents

1 Studying child development   1

2 Physical development   19

3 Perceptual development   39

4 Cognitive development   53

5 Language development   87

6 Personality and social development   111

   References   140

   Subject index   151

Acknowledgements

The author and publishers with to thank Harper and Row, London, for illustrations from G. Brown, D. H. Cherrington and L. Cohen. *Experiments in the social sciences.* (1975);

In addition the author wishes to express his thanks to Christine Brown and Charles Desforges for their advice on parts of the text.

1

Studying child development

Speculating on the way in which a child will grow up is probably an almost universal characteristic of adulthood, and may have been so for thousands of years. The observation that relatively helpless new-born infants will somehow become different, highly complex adults with many talents and perhaps many human failings is the activity from which the study of child development arises. Why do children develop uniquely? Can we influence that development? In what respects is a child of a certain age different from others of the same age? In what respects is he different from how he was when younger, or what he will become later? These are the questions which the student of child development seeks to answer. They are enormously weighty consider-ations, however, and one must be prepared for answers which are hesitant, speculatory or partial.

Historical Views of Development
Plato, in his Republic, described an ideal society which was based upon the inherited potentialities which he assumed each person to possess. These were such that people fell into one of three categories, those who were the artisans, with limited intellectual abilities, those who were capable of administering society, military personnel and civil servants, and finally the rulers. Plato recommended an educational regime which would cultivate the inherited intellectual skills of these rulers, or Philosopher Kings, so that they could rule with great wisdom.

The ideas of a Greek thinker of the fourth century B.C. may seem very remote, yet his views on the inherited potential of each individual and the manner in which society might foster it, are not too dissimilar from some which have been put forward in this century. Cyril Burt, a psychologist who gave evidence to The Consultative Committee on The

Primary School (1931) was quoted as saying that 'from quite early years, the degree of a child's intelligence roughly marks him out as fit for callings of a certain grade'. His view was hedged with qualifications, but the final report recommended schools of three types to follow the primary years, but they were not called schools for Artisans, Administrators and Philosopher Kings!

Jean Jacques Rousseau, writing in eighteenth century France, also assumed strong *innate*, or inherited, tendencies. In his view these tendencies were to *goodness* and *nobility*. The restrictive nature of contemporary society, he argued, had perverted the development of these fine qualities. Rousseau advocated a free and unrestrained environment which would enable the child, by active experiment and investigation, to develop into a healthy adult. This development would be orderly and sequential, moving through a series of stages, the end of which would be characterised by a particular view of the world.

Rousseau's work had an enormous impact upon educational thought. Pestalozzi in Switzerland, Montessori in Italy, and Dewey in America all advocated educational techniques which emphasised free environments in which the child could formulate his knowledge of reality. The concept of sequential stages in development is also an important aspect of the work of the Swiss psychologist, Jean Piaget (see Chapters 4 and 5).

One generation before Rousseau the English philosopher John Locke had taken a very different view. To him inheritance provided an organism with no qualities beyond certain animal-like movements. The mind was not endowed with any innate knowledge of good or evil. It contained only animal-like knowledge of needs and desires. With respect to the higher ideals of man it was a *tabula rasa*, a blank slate upon which experience would impress knowledge. As the 'blank slate' would record any kind of experience Locke exhorted educators to pay great attention to early experiences, so that they should not initiate trends which could not be halted. The animal-like 'self' must be controlled by educational experiences which encourage 'self-denial', 'self-discipline' and 'self-control'.

Locke's rejection of innate potential for these human qualities, and his description of development in terms of self-denial suggest that he did not see the child as different from the adult except in the quality of experience he had undergone. The child was an 'apprentice adult'. This view was not unique to Locke, it had a considerable history. Art historians point out that in earlier centuries children were portrayed as miniature adults, not with the proportions we now recognise as those of a child. In his book *Centuries of Childhood* Aries describes the child of the seventeenth century as not viewed with amusement and pleasure. He quotes a treatise by Balthazer Gratien as proclaiming that 'every man must be conscious of that insipidity of childhood which disgusts the sane mind; that coarseness of youth which finds pleasure in scarcely anything but material objects and which is only a very crude sketch of the man of thought'.

It can be seen that history has witnessed some remarkable differences in opinions of the nature of childhood. The views were principally those of philosophers, who, whilst being astute observers, evolved their theories in ways which may seem rather arbitrary to contemporary developmental psychologists. This is not to imply that contemporary social scientists do not disagree, but their disagreement is over the interpretation of data, or the manner in which it has been acquired, rather than abstract theorising about what it means to be human. Before embarking on a study of child development it is important that we clarify what social scientists mean by a theory and how they go about the business of formulating and testing it.

Theory and Experiment in Social Science

Whenever a psychologist turns his attention to some aspect of human behaviour he finds many ideas, opinions and myths already in existence. For instance, if he is interested in the development of speech he finds parents who believe their baby understands every word they say (as does the dog and the canary), many adults who refer to the baby's babbling as 'talking' and many adults who adopt simplified language and unusual or even bizarre vocabulary which they call 'baby talk'. He will do well to look at these layman's ideas carefully, for there is sometimes more than a germ of truth or reason in them. Furthermore the social scientist may have some of these notions from his own 'pre-scientific' background. He will also have certain biases in the type of social science he prefers. This may be dependent on many factors such as his own dispositions, the preferences of his teachers, and the breadth of his study and experience. He might wish to appear 'value-free'. That is, he would prefer to collect all the available data without bias. Unfortunately the supply of data is inexhaustable. He may concentrate his efforts on the environment in which the infant lives, or on the people in that environment, or he may eavesdrop on babbling when the baby is alone. He may even attempt to devise means of measuring movements of the vocal chords before birth. Whichever method he chooses tells us something of his bias, and most researchers accept that it is better to acknowledge this bias and to keep it within reasonable bounds rather than offer it as ammunition to critics of other persuasions.

Having explored the existing information, both from the layman and the professional, the developmental psychologist may then be in a position to formulate an *hypothesis*. An hypothesis is really a 'hunch' put in a way which makes it testable. Formulating an hypothesis serves two usesful functions; firstly, to synthesize the knowledge already gleaned into a prediction, and secondly, to give direction to subsequent investigations. To return to the example of language acquisition, the researcher may decide that human speech develops from copying others. This may be based on his observations that nearly all children learn to speak and that nearly all adults talk to infants long before they can respond with their own speech. His decision also tells us that his own bias is toward the effects of factors in the environment. So the hypothesis may be of the form:

Speed of acquisition of speech in infancy is directly related to the extent to which the child is exposed to adult speech.

This is now testable. To do so satisfactorily it is necessary to demonstrate that the relationship is *always* as predicted, and that it cannot be explained in any other way. If it was found that forty infants with superior speech at a given age had all been exposed to at least five hours adult speech per day, whereas forty infants with retarded speech had all had less than thirty minutes exposure per day, this would seem to confirm the hypothesis.

The researcher must be very cautious however, and before accepting confirmation of his hypothesis he must look carefully to ensure that there are no other explanations. What confounding factors might be involved in this deceptively simple relationship?

In the first place, the researcher has reported on 'infants', but we do not know whether they were boys or girls. Suppose that all the superior infants were girls and all the retarded ones were boys. The findings still support the original hypothesis, but they also support a rival hypothesis of the form:

Speed of acquisition of speech in infancy is greater in females than in males.

Now we do not know whether that is so because (i) girls have an innate, sex-linked potential which is superior to that of boys, or (ii) that adults respond verbally to girls more than to boys, or (iii) a mixture of these two.

There are many other possibilities. How many of each group had difficult or prolonged births? Do the adult language forms differ only in length? The reader can probably think of many others. The importance of indulging in this exercise is that it tells us how confident we may be about the researcher's conclusions. A good experiment is one in which the researcher attempts to eliminate all other possible explanations by controlling the factors involved. In our example he would have similar sex ratios in each group, he would ensure that all the infants had normal delivery, and he would attempt to show that the greatest differences were in the frequency of adult speech, not the quality of it.

Popper (1974) draws attention to the enormous power of refutation. Clearly we can only be *absolutely* certain of the language hypothesis if we test every living infant. However, if we test 1000, and in every case we find language performance related to exposure to adult speech (and if we have safeguarded against other explanations such as sex-linked inheritance) we might be confident that the hypothesis was confirmed. Yet a single instance of a child with superior language and no exposure to adult speech is sufficient to demolish the hypothesis. Such is the power of refutation. Total refutation is unlikely with this example, but it is highly possible that we may find an instance of a superior speaker with little exposure to adult speech. In this case we need not reject the hypothesis *in toto*, but we must modify it so that exposure to adult speech may be a contributory factor to speed of acquisition in infants; but we cannot accept it as a sole causal agent.

It should be noted that rejection of an hypothesis is not the same as confirmation of its converse. That is, although one child with no exposure to adult speech can lead to rejection of our hypothesis it may still be true that *for most children* exposure involves some hidden factor which is the crucial influence. What we must now do is hunt around to find out what that factor is, and how the one infant without exposure derived it from an alternate source.

The above example is of an hypothesis in its most accepted form. In psychological studies of development they are not always so precise. Sometimes descriptive surveys aim simply to discover what occurs at certain times in the life-cycle. Nevertheless, the same charges of bias and the same restrictions upon the validity of the findings must be recognised.

When an area has been investigated for some time there may be sufficient knowledge for the formulation of a theory. The word 'theory' is commonly used to denote all manner of things, hunches, guesses, opinions and suspicions; but a *scientific theory* is a statement of principles which organise existing knowledge of phenomena into an over-all explanatory system. Theory is not intended as a statement of *what exists*, but as a tool which helps us to imagine what is happening. It serves to expose the interrelationships between the fragments of knowledge which have been gained by observation and experiment.

Because a theory is a tool, not a description of what exists or occurs, we do not have to believe that which is 'true' and reject that which is 'false'. We judge a theory, as we would judge any tool, by how useful it is. Usually a theory which explains a large number of events is preferable to one of limited scope. In so doing it may involve notions which have not been tested. In a useful theory these can be tested and are open to refutation. A good theory will also be productive in the generation of new hypotheses for examination.

Research Design in Developmental Psychology

Developmental psychologists are interested in changes which occur systematically as the child gets older. A social psychologist may be interested in what happens to a child who moves from an isolated rural farm to an inner city terraced house. The change will, of course, take place over a period of time, even the most sophisticated social science cannot halt that, but it is the differences due to the change in social situation which interests him. The developmentalist, on the other hand, is interested in what happens over that period of time if the social situation does not vary. His concern is whether six-year-olds respond differently from seven-year-olds in *any* social setting. Unfortunately age cannot be isolated as a factor for experimental manipulation. The seven-year-old is not simply one year older. He is generally stronger, taller and has a whole year of additional experience of life. His greater mobility may give him a larger group of friends, so to some extent the social and developmental psychologists do examine the same phenomena, but their emphases are different.

To commence any study the researcher needs a group of children, for he cannot hope to assess all the children in an age range. This poses an immediate problem, for he needs to be able to *generalise* his findings, that is, to conclude with reasonable certainty that what he has observed in his group will be true of all such children. If he has studied only boys, or only working class children, he cannot make that assumption. To obviate this experimental group must be a *sample* which represents the whole *universe* of children of that age. In drawing a sample of several hundred schoolchildren from all those in a large city and its surrounding countryside it may be satisfactory to draw a random sample, that is, draw names out of a hat. If smaller samples are necessary the researcher may have deliberately to include certain categories of children so that the sample represents the whole universe in, say, the proportion of working class and middle class, the proportion of boys and girls, and the distribution of children of different intelligence levels. This is not difficult with such obvious factors, but in many relatively ill-defined areas confounding factors may not be recognised until the study is completed. Nevertheless, developmental psychologists treat with caution findings which are based upon obviously biased samples.

Social scientists cannot often choose their samples freely, but must select them from a pool of volunteers. This may be a source of bias too. It is relatively easy to imagine that parents who volunteer their infants as subjects for a study may be different in some important ways from those who do not. They may have more time, they may have read a good deal about child development, or they may be hoping to get free expert opinion on their own offspring. The possibilities are endless.

An invaluable safeguard in experimental work is the use of *replication*. If researchers using other samples obtain similar results the findings can be accepted with greater confidence. Unfortunately replication is much less extensive in the social sciences than the natural sciences, partly by tradition, and partly because, as we have seen, it is often extremely difficult to determine exactly which factors in a given situation are crucial, and hence to replicate the study exactly.

The usual method of counteracting the vagaries of everyday life, such as moving home, breaking a leg, losing a parent, or gaining a sister, is to examine a sample of children of a specified age. Accidental changes are less likely to show up in the average behaviour of a group. The most obvious method of determining age-related differences is to gather a sample of, say, three-year-olds and assess behaviours at six-monthly intervals for a number of years. This is called a *longitudinal* study.

Longitudinal studies are necessarily lengthy, at least as long as the time spent under investigation plus an additional year or more for planning and analysing the results. During the study a proportion of the sample may be lost either because families move or because participants lose interest. This is more hazardous than may appear at first sight, for such *attrition* is seldom random. Families moving from the area are more likely to be from the middle class so that early assessments of younger children from both social classes have to be compared with later assessments from a biased sample.

The major advantage of the lengthy longitudinal study is that it enables the researcher to assess the actual rates at which individual children develop. The average information derived from the group can be obtained by other means, but only by following individual children over a period of time is it possible to comment upon the differences in *rates* of development and to examine the characteristics of those who develop speedily or tardily.

Longitudinal studies are also the most reliable means of testing certain cause-and-effect hypotheses. If one wishes to examine the hypothesis that strong motivation to achieve is dependent upon parental behaviour during infancy, this can only be done reliably by designing a category system for recording parental behaviour, recording the results, and waiting until the children grow old enough to display achievement striving behaviour, perhaps at the age of ten. An alternative is to assess achievement striving in ten-year-olds and ask them or their parents questions about how the parents behaved during the child's infancy. As one might imagine reminiscence by parents and children's subjective assessments of their infancy are extremely unreliable.

A more common research method is one which takes different samples of children of different ages, and compares them. This is known as a *cross-sectional* study. Because one is comparing the average development or performance of a sample of, say, six-year-olds with that of a sample of ten-year-olds, the research process can be speeded up enormously. Most of the developmental information available has been obtained by this means. If we require to know the average height of boys at six years and ten years this method is entirely adequate, providing all the usual sampling requirements have been met. If, on the other hand, we wish to know whether the boy who is exceptionally tall at six years of age will still be so as a ten-year-old, we must turn to longitudinal studies for our answer. Figure 1.1 represents the differences between these two forms of research with some imaginary data.

Both of these studies indicate that the average height has increased by 30 cms between the ages of six and ten years. If these samples were much

Longitudinal study

Child	height at 6 years (cm)	Child	height at 10 years (cm)
Adam	105	Adam	125
Barry	115	Barry	145
Colin	125	Colin	165
Average	115	Average	145

Cross-sectional study

Child	height at 6 years (cm)	Child	height at 10 years (cm)
Adam	105	Donald	125
Barry	115	Eric	145
Colin	125	Fred	165
Average	115	Average	145

Figure 1.1 Longitudinal and cross-sectional data

larger, and were truly representative of *all* children of these ages we could also infer that at six years of age there is less variability in height than at ten years (a range of 20 cms at six years and 40 cms at ten years).

If that is the information we seek, the cross-sectional study will suffice. Both age *cohorts* (representative samples) could be assessed at the same time. The longitudinal study must take four years because we have to wait for Adam, Barry and Colin to become ten years old. The additional value of this study is that we can obtain information of the rates of development of *individuals*. Adam, who was the shortest at six years is still the shortest at ten. He has increased by only one half of Colin's gain. In the cross-sectional study we have no way of determining whether Donald was small at six years, so we can predict nothing of Adam's rate of growth.

These data are entirely fictitious and are invented to illustrate the differences between the two studies. For an accurate summary of growth trends the reader should consult Tanner (1961, 1978).

Research Methods

To measure (accurately) the height of children may require apparatus a little more sophisticated than a tape-measure, but it can hardly be regarded as a technological problem. Physical growth can be assessed in a variety of ways, however, and some of these may be quite complex, such as assessments of blood volume or the degree to which the skeleton has become ossified (see Chapter 2).

All these are relatively straightforward in comparison with assessments of behaviour. That which looks most like the use of a 'tape-measure' is the use of *standardised tests* for the measurement of personality, intelligence or performance of a skill.

The best known of the varieties is probably the intelligence test, which is designed to assess the intellectual potential of an individual, independent of the amount he has learned.

There are many published forms of these I.Q. tests, most of them available in a range suitable for subjects between the ages of five years and adulthood. They have been carefully tested to ensure their suitability for the age in question, and precise instructions are given so that everyone is presented with the same situation. Some of them are written questions and answers, these are called verbal intelligence tests. Others, the non-verbal tests, rely upon manipulation of objects or selection of abstract geometric symbols and patterns. With very young children even the ability to manipulate an object or hold a pencil may be suspect. In such cases procedures are usually adopted which assess what the child's physical capabilities are. These are usually referred to as developmental tests.

Intelligence tests are most widely used to check on the representativeness of samples in developmental studies. They can be used to assess changes in intelligence with age, but because tests have to be 'tailored' specifically for children of a given age, such comparative procedures are hazardous, particularly in the early years.

Standardised tests have an important place in psychology, but they are not without their critics. Whilst intelligence is theoretically a notion of potential or capability, in practice it must be assessed by performance, or what the subject can do. It is therefore inevitable that learning will have some effect upon its assessment. Similarly, in assessing personality the subject is often asked to report his own behaviour, and a variety of factors may affect the accuracy of this report. Saying how one would behave in given circumstances is not the same as doing it.

Whilst standardised tests may be used in selecting samples, they are less often used as a part of the research procedure in developmental psychology. Often the behaviours under investigation are so varied and complex that they are simply not amenable to such assessment procedures. The researcher may then attempt to record the actual behaviours as they occur.

Earlier the problem of observer bias was broached. In observing and recording actual child behaviours it may be quite prominent. Even the observer who attempts to record all he sees is limited by his own capacities. If he records all a child's behaviours, verbal and non-verbal, should he also record details of the environment? Children react to objects, people and events, and at some stage the observer will have to decide which are pertinent, for he cannot record them all. Even a T.V. camera is biased by the cameraman who points it.

Observations of children's natural behaviours may be continuous over quite long periods of time. In such studies it is usually the observer's intention to describe the types of behaviour he observed and the frequency of their occurrence. Often the observations have to be recorded and classified in the actual situation, by a researcher at the back of the classroom, for instance. In these cases *time sampling* may be employed. Here a brief period of behaviour is recorded at regular intervals. The length of each period and the interval is calculated so that there is a good chance of the over-all assessment being a fairly accurate representation of the total distribution of behaviours by the child throughout that period. Apart from reducing the load on the observer it can be used to allow an observer systematically to record the behaviours of a number of children in a group, by shifting attention from child to child at regular intervals.

As we have seen, observation of naturally occurring behaviour does not preclude bias, but it is believed to give a realistic impression of child behaviours. The justification for this belief with regard to time sampling is that most of the more frequent behaviours are likely to be represented. However, critics point out that the frequency of an event may not always be the best indicator of its importance. For example, a child may be smacked once by another child, and this may occur between time samples observed by the researcher. Yet in spite of being a single event it might be crucial to understanding all subsequent behaviours on that day. Only continuous observation would be likely to detect this.

Researchers who are concerned with only one type of behaviour would restrict their records to that type of event. Furthermore, they may structure the situation in order to detect changes in behaviour. This procedure is known as *controlled observation*. Smith, Connolly and Fleming (1972) used such a technique to investigate children's behaviours when the quantity of play equipment and the size of play area were systematically varied.

The aim of naturalistic observation is to describe behaviour. The aim of controlled observation may be that, or may be to test an hypothesis about certain influences on behaviour. Varying situational factors may lead to changes in behaviour which may be explained in a variety of ways. In Smith, Connolly and Fleming's study one cannot be sure whether changes which took place when the play area was reduced were due to diminished space and/or closer proximity of playmates and/or increased danger of accident and/or the children's perceptions of being enclosed and cramped and/or sudden inexplicable changes to their play group. Their observations are none-the-less interesting and may be important to play group planners, but psychologists may wish to know rather more about exactly *why* changes have occurred. To answer this question researchers may have to adopt a much stricter *experimental method*, involving formulation of precise hypotheses, and systematic control of other variables which are not involved in the hypotheses (see p14).

Controlled experiment may seem to be the epitome of psychological research, but, like everything else, it has its weaknesses. One of the most serious, paradoxically, may be the high degree of control which is exercised. The reader may recall our speculative hypothesis relating the speed with which an infant acquired language and exposure to adult speech. To test this the researcher should control the likelihood of some adults talking, smiling and gesturing whilst others simply speak in a monotone, he should also control the quantity of 'baby talk' in the adult utterances. Yet by so doing he may confirm his hypothesis in a scientific, though thoroughly unlifelike manner. That is, he might show that, 'other things being equal' the exposure to adult speech is related to speed of acquisition by infants, but may have 'controlled out' the fact that one hour of animated speech with laughter, gesture, expression is superior to five hours of dreary monotone. In other words, there is a grave danger that the tight control necessary in an experimental study may provide findings with little utility in real life. Whilst this criticism is not without merit, the confirmation of the hypothesis does not preclude the confirmation of other hypotheses related to it, and many experimental studies are substantially more sophisticated than that outlined here. In these it is often possible to ascertain quite complex interrelationships between variables, each affecting the speed of acquisition to some degree.

Contemporary Developmental Psychology

The burgeoning of psychological studies of human development is a twentieth century phenomenon. The previous section attested to techniques which were principally descriptive, and others which were experimental. The earliest studies were largely of the former variety, detailed descriptions of the sequential organisation of motor activities and the average ages at which they occurred. Subsequently experimental techniques which were proving effective in other areas of psychology were brought in to investigate specific mechanisms. With their intrusion the emphasis tended to swing from interest in physical and motor development to learning, perception and language. No doubt developmental psychology will witness the decline and resurgence of particular interests in the future. The varied interests of practitioners are indicative of more than one goal.

Ausubel and Sullivan (1970) pointed out that these different types of study had different objectives. The descriptive study might be concerned with the behaviour of children at different ages, *per se* – its purpose being to extract growth trends as 'yardsticks' against which a child could be measured. Alternatively the 'objective' assessment of development may be only a preliminary step toward identifying the 'subjective' impact of that change upon the individual. For instance the mean age at which girls in Britain first menstruate is about thirteen years. This information enables us to determine whether a particular girl is an early developer. On the other hand it does not tell us whether the girl perceives herself as such, though it suggests we might seek that further evidence as a possible cause of her social behaviours.

Whatever emphasis we choose, the concept of *development* presupposes some sort of *orderly continuity* in the changes that are recorded. Interest in this continuity lead developmentalists to consider the possible existence of *innate features* of human beings as well as *environmental features*. There are three aspects of this maxim which deserve closer attention, for they will reappear in many guises in subsequent chapters.

Development: Maturation and Learning

As a baby develops from a single fertilised egg he absorbs nutrients, firstly from his mother's blood, later from her milk and then from ordinary food. The food is broken down by his body and used to repair damage to tissues, to generate energy and to enable body cells to multiply. This process of multiplication is *growth*. The single fertilised egg does not simply divide into a mass of cells, however; nor does an infant simply grow into a larger, adult version. Hand-in-hand with growth go the processes of *development*.

Development may be described as the changes of form or function which occur over time, usually, though not invariably, in accompaniment with growth. The mass of eggs in the womb grows. It also develops a special shape, and cells from different regions become modified to perform different functions in the gut, the skin, the brain, etc. The infant bicep enlarges as the child grows older and the degree of control over it enables arm movements to develop in precision and complexity.

The development of the mass of cells into a recognisable foetus occurs without any conscious activity by the cells. Similarly the development of adult sexual characteristics which accompanies growth to adult size is triggered by some internal mechanism. These developments are the result of *maturation*. On the other hand, changes in behaviour may develop from the particular activities which an individual performs. Strength of the bicep and degree of manual dexterity depend very much upon the extent to which the individual has had opportunities to exercise in appropriate situations. They are the results of *learning*.

Heredity and Environment

The extent to which a particular form of behaviour is dependent upon innate or learned factors is quite important to society. If we are to assume that, say, aggression is dependent upon inborn characteristics, we may feel that the activities of aggressive people should be restricted but that there is little we can do to change them; 'it's in the blood' older generations might have said. If we take the view that a person has *become* aggressive because of certain learning experiences we may feel more optimistic. We can try to avoid exposing children to those experiences and we could try to get aggressive people to learn more acceptable behaviours. Such debates are often referred to as *nature-nurture* controversies.

Some of the earlier developmental theories had particular biases in favour of one side or the other. *Nativist* theories emphasised the genetic and maturational aspects of human development. They contrasted with those *empiricist* theories which proposed that development was principally a matter of exploring the environment and learning behaviours by interaction with it.

Differing views of the origins of intelligence have given rise to one form of what is sometimes called a nature-nurture controversy. On one side (Eysenck, 1971; Jensen, 1969) evidence has been marshalled to suggest that inheritance is the major determinant of the differences in intelligence which exist between individuals. Opposers (Richardson and Spears, 1972; Kamin, 1974) take the environmentalist view. In fact it is rather misleading to cast the debate in such an extreme form. The argument is really about the relative weight of inherited and learned influences. Nor is the controversy about 'whether intelligence is inherited or derived from the environment'. Both factors are clearly essential for the growth and development of any feature of an organism. The argument is about the attribution of cause to different levels of intelligence, and is represented by the debate between Eysenck and Kamin (1981).

It is becoming increasingly clear that both inheritance and learning are involved in most developmental processes. Earlier it was stated that the onset of puberty was a maturational phenomenon. So it is, but we know that environment, in the form of malnutrition or anxiety, may delay it. Similarly it was asserted that bicep strength was due to learning, in the form of exercise. So it is, but there is also an inherited influence. Muscular children are likely to come from parents of good physique. Because of the growing awareness of the interaction between these two factors, more and more contemporary developmental psychologists are querying the relevance of nature-nurture controversies. Weighing the relative influences is rather like asking 'if bread requires 2 lbs of flour and 1 oz of yeast, which ingredient is the more important?' It is perhaps more appropriate to assume interaction between the two and concern ourselves with the description of the environment and the precise way in which the individual interacts with it.

Developmental Stages
Within the overall pattern of interacting environmental and inherited

factors it is possible to generate developmental theories which have very general applicability. A learning theory which assumed certain innate predispositions for mimicry can be used to explain the development of social responses, physical skills and intellectual behaviour at any time in the life cycle. Alternatively a theory can espouse a rather more complex pattern of innate predispositions in which the organism becomes sensitised to different aspects of the environment at different periods of life. Both Sigmund Freud and Jean Piaget have elaborated theories based upon this concept. Such theories are called *stage theories* because they require special modes of explanation for each phase of development.

The danger of forming too rigid a concept of stages is just as great as that of seeing nature-nurture as two mutually exclusive alternatives. Basically stage theories suggest that innate mechanisms cause the new-born infant to interact with his environment in certain ways which provide him with a complement of knowledge and related skills. These are all characterised by being formed in this 'certain way' and will have some features in common.

This complement of knowledge and skills forms the basis on which the next stage can be built as development causes new processes to be brought into operation. Because each stage forms the base from which the next stage emerges the *sequence* of stages is fixed. That is, Stage 2 is such that it develops from the knowledge and skills of Stage 1. It cannot precede Stage 1, and Stage 3 cannot follow Stage 1 because it depends upon the skills and knowledge of Stage 2.

Frequently the stages of a particular theory are linked to specific ages, for example, Stage 1 (0-1 years), Stage 2 (1-2 years) etc. It is important to remember that these are rough estimates based upon the time the average child takes to master the various stages, and the approximate age at which maturational changes occur.

Some critics (see Flavell, 1975) have reacted against the 'static' view of development which stages are sometimes seen to imply. That is, the view that when an individual is 'in' a stage he continues behaving in a specified way until he shifts rather abruptly into the next stage. This model is illustrated in Figure 1.2(a). Stage 1 is achieved 'instantaneously' and maintained until the sudden acquisition of Stage 2 and then Stage 3. A rather more realistic interpretation is shown in Figure 1.2(b). Here the acquisition of a stage is seen as occurring over a considerable period of time. When it is fully acquired, or nearly so, the individual has the requirements for the next stage, which immediately begins to develop.

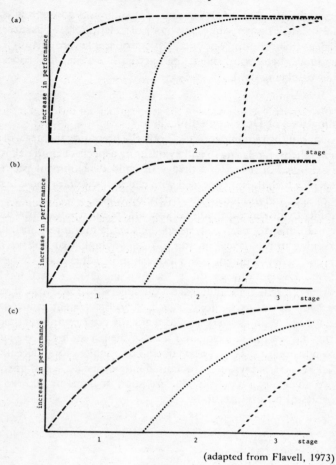

(adapted from Flavell, 1973)

Figure 1.2 Interpretations of stages

Flavell prefers an even more gradual model, as illustrated in Figure 1.2(c). In this view the concept of stage is even more vague and diffuse. It can be defined only in terms of those characteristic attributes which are newly emerging, and it will overlap substantially with more advanced developments of earlier stages. This change in emphasis points out the nature of a scientific theory as it was described earlier. The very naive stage theory would have to be rejected if evidence was presented showing that the behaviour of individuals could contain a mixture of characteristics from different stages. Flavell's alternative shows quite clearly that the notion of a stage is a conceptual tool, a means of labelling a predominant mode of functioning, whilst accepting the idea that at any one time a considerable proportion of an individual's behaviour might be 'atypical' within the conceptual framework being used.

Applications of Developmental Theory

Throughout the remainder of this book the preceding themes will recur in many theories relating to widely differing aspects of child behaviour. The existence of a credible theory of child development provides a means by which those concerned with children's welfare and education may predict and influence future development.

Ability to influence a child's behaviours raises an issue with which we have not, hitherto, been concerned. This is the moral responsibility of intervening in the developmental process. Whether or not we *should* intervene in development is not a question which is open to the same sort of investigations as those seeking factual information. Some researchers might argue that this is a question which is beyond the scope of developmental psychology. Psychology, they might argue, should collect the facts and society should make the decisions about their use. Yet this may be too convenient a way for the psychologist to shake off his responsibilities. True, he has no claim to make moral decisions for his fellow men, but with his specialised knowledge he is, perhaps, better able to advise society on the interpretation of the facts and the likely outcomes of certain decisions.

2

Physical Development

The human body is made up of cells. They may take a variety of forms, depending upon their function (e.g. blood cells, nerve cells, bone cells, etc.) but their internal composition is fairly uniform. The surface of the cell is covered with a membrane, and within the membrane is a substance known as cytoplasm. Within the cytoplasm is a denser area known as the nucleus which contains twenty-three pairs of bodies called chromosomes (Figure 2/1). Chromosomes are minute, thread-like particles which are themselves made up of smaller units known as genes. There is strong evidence that genes consist of complex molecules which, joined together, form a spiral of deoxyribonucleic acid (DNA) which is the chromosome (Watson and Crick, 1953). The genes carry the blueprint for the development of the individual by organising growth and specifying the role of cells.

As the human body grows the number of cells increases. This is accomplished by a process known as *mitosis*. Each of the forty-six chromosomes splits in half, the halves move to opposite sidesof the cell and the cell then divides, producing two identical daughter cells (Figure 2/2).

Hereditary Transmission
The only exceptions to the general cell structure described above are the *germ cells*. These are the sperms and ova (eggs) produced by the reproductive organs. In their development the final phase involves the separation of the pairs of chromosomes, with one whole chromosome of each pair going into each germ cell (or *gamete*). At conception a gamete from the man fuses with one from the woman thus producing a *zygote*, a 'typical' cell with a full complement of forty-six chromosomes again.

There is no way of determining which chromosomes from each pair will be present in either the ovum or the sperm, nor is there any way of determining which one of the millions of sperms will impregnate the

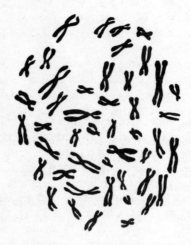

Figure 2.1 Chromosomes greatly magnified

(a) ribbon-like chromosomes   (b) chromosomes shorten and thicken

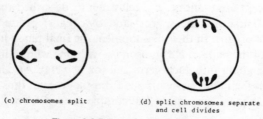

(c) chromosomes split   (d) split chromosomes separate
and cell divides

Figure 2.2 Principal stages in mitosis

ovum released by the woman. It is this random assortment which accounts for the fact that children of the same parents often do not look much alike, and why they resemble their parents to only a limited extent.

Immediately following fertilisation the zygote will begin to grow and divide until a mass of cells exists in place of the original one. Over a period of time these undifferentiated cells will begin to take on specialised forms until eventually an embryo is developed containing many of the recognisable organs of the human body. After eighteen days the embryo is about one-fifth of an inch long. At two months it will be about 1 inch long, and by this time most anatomical features will be visible. At this stage it becomes a foetus. In order for this rapid development to take place it is essential that the intra-uterine environment should be satisfactory. Should the foetus fail to be nourished, or should the amniotic fluid within the uterus be contaminated, there is a possibility of malformation. Thus, even at this very early stage, we are faced not with a developmental pattern based entirely upon genetic make-up, but upon the complex interaction between that given pattern and the environment in which it operates.

Although we usually think of the parents as possessing all the genes which make up the offspring there is also a possibility that a zygote will contain some genetic material which is quite different from that donated by either the mother or the father. Such a chance alteration is known as a mutation. Often mutations are damaging to development and many mutated foetuses will be still-born or will fail to develop in the uterus. However from time to time it may be that such a mutation will come to full-term pregnancy and will be born and it is these chance alterations which are thought to be important developments in the history of species. In the Darwinian theory of evolution the existence of a new form, if more appropriately adapted to existing conditions, will survive more successfully, old forms will die out and an evolutionary development will have taken place in that species. Nash (1970) speculates that telepathic communication could change the human species if such a mutation was possible, although in fairness he admits that the idea is more in keeping with science fiction than developmental psychology.

Genetic and Environmental Influences

There are some aspects of the developing individual which are clearly

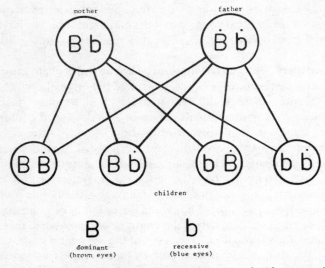

Figure 2.3 Possible genetic endowment of offspring of parents each with one recessive gene

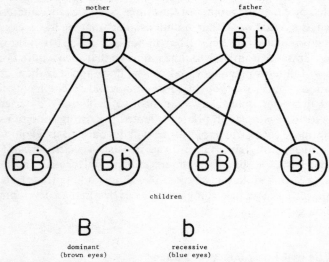

Figure 2.4 Possible genetic endowment of offspring of parents, one of whom has two dominant genes

attributable to the action of genes. An example of this is eye colour. The gene for brown eyes is dominant and will exert its influence over the gene for blue eyes, which is said to be recessive. Thus if the individual inherits a dominant brown eye gene from the mother and a similar gene from the father it will carry two dominant genes and will have brown eyes. If it inherits a dominant gene from one parent and a recessive or blue eyed gene from the other it will still have brown eyes as the brown gene is dominant. In the presence of two recessive genes the individual will have blue eyes. The possibilities of the pairings of genes are shown in Figure 2.3. The diagram represents the genes of two parents each having brown eyes but carrying a dominant brown eyed and a recessive blue eyed gene. The possibility of a blue eyed child from this parentage can be seen to be one in four. Of course if either of the brown eyed parents had a genetic constitution consisting of two dominant genes then the offspring would have brown eyes as it would always carry one of these dominant genes (Figure 2.4).

With the exception of the reproductive cells all the cells in the female body consist of twenty-two pairs of chromosomes which are similar to those present in the male. Such chromosomes are sometimes called autosomes. The twenty-third pair are different in that in the female they consist of two like chromosomes called X chromosomes. In the male this twenty-third pair consists of one X chromosome and one Y chromosome. As germ cells contain only one half of the twenty-three pairs i.e. twenty-three single chromosomes, every ovum produced by the female will contain one X chromosome, whereas in the male the sperm may contain the X chromosome or a Y chromosome. If the X chromosome from the female pairs with an X chromosome from the male the offspring will be female. If it pairs with a Y chromosome from the male the offspring will be male. The possible relationships between these are shown in Figure 2.5.

Although we know that the basic gender of the individual is dependent upon this relatively simple mechanism it is incorrect to assume that psychological characteristics which a culture may typically associate with the different sexes, for example the submissiveness and domesticated characteristic of the female and the aggressive characteristic of the male, are direct results of this difference. Evidence suggests that the psychological attributes are reinforced by the culture and have little to do with inheritance. However not all the evidence is of this nature and there is some suggestion that there may be certain inherited differences between the sexes, though these will be highly influenced by

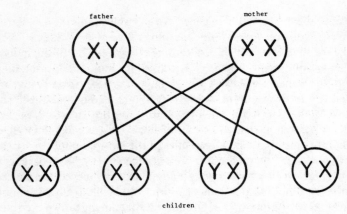

Figure 2.5 Parental sex chromosomes and possible gender of offspring

cultural pressures (see Chapter 6).

Differences in level of intelligence between individuals are, as we have already seen, considered by some researchers to be attributable to inherited factors whilst others emphasise cultural influences. It should be noted that the evidence which is used in this argument is of a much less direct nature than that previously mentioned for eye colour or sex. There is little indication at present that specific genes are implicated in the development of intelligence and it is commonly assumed that such features are probably dependent on highly complex interactions of a multiplicity of genes.

The interpretation of gene action given above is very simple and indeed psychological use of genetic explanations has tended to be of this simple-minded nature. It is important to realise however that gene interaction is a highly complex affair. All genes seem to have numerous actions; that is, whilst we can sometimes clearly locate the principal result of a gene action, there is evidence to suggest that the same gene may be implicated in many other mechanisms within the organism. Similarly the gene from one parent may interact with a gene from the other to produce an action of which there was no indication in either parent. Some genes, known as modifier genes, have a modifying effect upon the action of others. Thus gene A may determine whether a particular characteristic is present in the infant but gene B may determine exactly how that characteristic will be manifest. For example, the presence of cataracts on the cornea of the eye is known to be due to a simple dominant gene, but the degree of opacity of those cataracts is thought to be influenced by the presence of other modifier genes.

The situation is further complicated by the phenomenon of *penetrance*. Penetrance refers to the frequency with which a particular genetic constitution causes actual changes in the structure and/or behaviour of individuals. This can be referred to as the frequency with which *genotype* (the actual genetic constitution) corresponds to *phenotype* (how the individual appears or behaves). A genotype of 60 per cent penetrance would be one in which, out of every 100 individuals with that genetic constitution, sixty would display the characteristic (see below). But of those sixty who did show the characteristic there is the added possibility that they may show it to different degrees. This is known as the *expressivity* of the genotype.

Twin Studies

Differences in penetrance and expressivity can often be seen in identical twins. These twins have both developed from the same fertilised ovum: the fertilised egg has split and developed into two similar organisms. As it comes from the same zygote these twins are called *monozygous* twins. It is not uncommon to find monozygous twins who manifest quite different levels of the same abnormality, i.e. one with severe diabetes, the other with only a very minor affliction of the same ailment. In such cases it is assumed that differences in the environments of the twins have 'triggered off' the deficiency in different ways, though it is usually only possible to speculate on what these differences in the environment are. For instance if one of these twins had had a predilection for sweets and had eaten large quantities of sugar during his childhood or had suffered a severe shock which the other had not, this environmental factor may have triggered off a mechanism which was already potentially there in his genetic make-up. The case of identical twins is a particularly interesting one for the developmental psychologist trying to establish the nature of the complex interaction between genetic constitution and environment. However, to simply classify monozygous twins as having identical genetic make-up is a dangerous occupation. Evidence suggests that in rare cases the fertilised ovum does not split uniformly. Sheinfeld (1973) describes some of the more unusual occurrences during this splitting. Added to this is the complication that the immediate environment in the uterus may not itself be entirely equivalent. The actual siting of the foetus in the placenta could have dramatic effects upon the level of nutriment which the foetus receives. Giving due regard to these problems there is, nevertheless, considerable evidence that the degree of similarity in physical and mental traits of identical twins is very much higher than would have been achieved in siblings or unrelated children. Mittler (1971) in an extensive review of data confirms this view, but cautions that developmental rates for twins tend to be retarded and therefore direct comparisons with single children may be misleading.

Genetic Causes of Abnormality

Genetic abnormalities frequently cause foetal death. However, as medical techniques become more sophisticated it becomes increasingly possible to keep abnormal individuals alive and in some cases to enable them to breed. There is a particular moral problem involved in this situation in which a gene pool which would normally have been kept relatively uniform by the early death of abnormal individuals may now become increasingly biased by abnormal individuals' contributions. Such a problem is one for society as a whole and not particularly for the developmental psychologist. For the student of child development there are some common genetic abnormalities which occur in the population and which are found in children in schools and hospitals.

Down's Syndrome (a form of what was previously known as Mongolism) is caused by an extra chromosome in the cells of the individual. It is frequently, though not exclusively, caused by atypical ova in the mother, and is related to maternal age. Whilst a mother of twenty-five years has only one chance in 2000 of producing a child with this condition, a forty-five year old mother has one chance in 40 (Illingworth, 1966). The term "mongol" was one that was used for many years to describe a condition characterised by a flat nose, thick lips with protruding tongue, slant eyes and coarse skin and hair. It was once thought to give a resemblance to the Mongol race, though this is quite erroneous. The extent of the abnormal physical features and the severity of the concomitant intellectual deficit is subject to remarkable variations. Increasingly educators are becoming aware that a Down's child is by no means necessarily ineducable, and indeed very great gains in social and intellectual development have been achieved with some of these children (Gulliford, 1971). Examination of a group of these children demonstrates the variation of expressivity of genetic deficit. Some children will be hardly distinguishable from their normal peers whereas others will be quite clearly severely handicapped.

About one adult in every 200 of the population carries a recessive gene which contributes to a condition known as phenylketonuria (PKU). Because it is a recessive gene there is a very low likelihood that such an individual will marry a partner with a similar defective gene. Occasionally this happens however and a defective child may be born. This unfortunate condition clearly indicates a close interaction which occurs between genotype and the environment in the production of the phenotype. Individuals suffering from PKU are unable to convert certain chemicals in their food into a form which can be absorbed by the body. The chemical in question is phenylalinine which is normally converted by the liver into tyrosine. In this condition the liver is unable to complete this conversion and the body becomes saturated with phenylinine. Some of this is removed through the urine but a proportion of it remains in the body and this proportion gradually increases until the body is saturated with the substance. This causes a blocking of the normal nerve pathways in the body and so an apparently normal infant gradually develops into an abnormal child with progressive signs of mental deficiency. The condition cannot be cured in the sense that the defective genes can be altered. It can however be 'cured' in another sense in that the genes can only operate in an adequate environment; an environment which provides phenylalinine in the diet. By carefully controlling the diet to eliminate this chemical the individual can develop normally. It must be pointed out that this is only one cause of mental deficiency and is known to be present in only a very small proportion of those who are so characterised. There is little evidence that other gene abnormalities are the causes of the many other forms of mental deficiency which are observed in the population.

The intra-uterine environment has its own interaction with the genotype of the individual and it is therefore not uncommon for children to be born with deficiencies from this source. The blood type of the foetus determined by the interaction of gene patterns from the sperm and the ovum may be different from that of the mother. Normally this does not matter, but in certain cases the leakage of maternal blood into the circulatory system of the foetus can prove a hazard. This condition, known as haemolytic incompatibility, may occur when a mother with blood of the rhesus negative type carries a child with rhesus positive blood inherited from the father's dominant genes. If rhesus positive blood cells leak from the foetus into the placenta they will be attacked by the mother's system as though they were foreign bodies.

In consequence the mother's blood develops antibodies to protect her from further invasion. These antibodies can pass with other fluids from the mother into the foetus thereby effectively injecting it with substances which will destroy its blood cells. The resulting condition may vary from a mild form of jaundice in the new born child to a very severe condition known as kernicterus in which there is severe mental abnormality and considerable physical deformity due to abnormal muscular contractions and rigidity of the body. Fortunately such a condition is not an automatic consequence of the mating of the rhesus positive father with the rhesus negative mother. Firstly, the child will not always inherit a rhesus positive blood system; secondly, there may be no leakage; thirdly, haemolytic incompatability can now be determined early in pregnancy and adequate safe-guards taken.

Growth and Development

It was noted that from the time of conception two things were occurring simultaneously to the zygote. Firstly, it was multiplying so that increasing numbers of cells were produced within the uterus. Secondly, the form of the cells was changing so that different parts of the foetus were becoming differentiated for different purposes. Two somewhat similar mechanisms can be seen throughout the rest of childhood. At one level there is an increase in the body bulk, in the quantity of tissues such as skeleton and muscle and this can properly be called the growth of the organism. Hand in hand with this goes increasing sophistication in the use of the body. This can be called development. Taking the span of childhood as a whole it will be obvious that these two processes are very closely allied so that we would expect the increasing size of a limb or an organ to be progressing in parallel with increasing development. However this is not always so; it may be that increased size or greater musculature may not signify increasing sophistication of use. An early developing three-year-old may have fingers the size of those of an average six-year-old, but may lack the manipulative ability. From the point of view of the developmental psychologist it may be important to know whether a specific task presented to the child is demanding simply a certain level of growth or whether it also requires a particular level of development.

A number of general theories have been elaborated on the way in which development and growth occurs. One such theory is that the direction of development is governed by a *cephalocaudal principle*. This takes as evidence that the head of the foetus is larger and better developed than its legs and that in the development of the foetus arm buds appear before leg buds. In similar fashion improvements in visual coordination tend to precede the use of hands and this in turn precedes the use of legs and feet. This *cephalocaudal principle* proposes that the development trend is from the head down to the feet.

It has also been observed that sequence of development in the arms proceeds from the shoulder to the arm to the hand to the fingers. This sequence and similar sequences give rise to the *proximodistal principle*, which states that growth and development proceed from the central vertical axis of the body outwards. Until quite recently observations of the infant's ability to reach out and grasp an object suggested that the early stages of movement were of a gross motor nature deriving from the large muscles of the shoulder and arm. Subsequently the action becomes more precise and directional, and latterly the fingers and thumb come to be used for fine manipulation. Similarly the toddler tends to walk clumsily using mostly muscles of the upper arms and upper legs. After a period of time the use of lower parts of the limbs allows the walking to be more fluid and precise.

A third principle which to some extent espouses aspects of the two former principles is that the movement of the young child tends to be dependent in its early stages upon the use of large muscles and that increasing refinement bring into operation finer movements. Thus the principle here is that the development is from the use of gross mass to specific activities. Recent studies involving the detailed analysis of behaviour patterns of new-born and very young infants (Bower, 1974) cast some doubt upon the accuracy of these foregoing descriptions. He claims that quite accurate reaching and grasping behaviour can be seen in children of only a few weeks of age.

In general, principles such as those elaborated above have proved to have little utility in the study of child development. In recent times emphasis has been placed upon more accurate descriptions of normative development in the child and in trying to ascertain the causes of abnormalities. In this respect considerable interest has been aroused in whether specific aspects of behaviour can be considered to be dependent upon maturation of the organism or on learning from the environment. If development of motor abilities is dependent upon internal processes then we need not be too concerned with the type of environment which is present to the child during this period. If, on the other hand, the type of environment in which the child finds himself has a drastic effect upon the type of motor development which he will manifest then this is of great importance. A completely environmental learning theory would suggest that, if the environment does not provide appropriate forms of stimulation no development will occur in that area until such time as it is presented. Bower discusses the evidence on this point and in particular refers to studies on the smiling response in infants. At a chronological age of six weeks the normal infant will smile at an appropriate visual stimulus. If we add to this six weeks the forty weeks for which the child was in the uterus we can say that this child has a conceptual age of forty-six weeks, in other words for forty-six weeks this child has been receptive to input from an environment of one sort or another. We can then compare the age at which smiling occurs in infants born prematurely or post-term. A child born after thirty-six weeks gestation would, after a further six weeks, have only a conceptual age of forty-two weeks, whereas one born four weeks over full-term would have a conceptual age of fifty weeks. Bower concludes that the evidence strongly suggests that infants smile at a conceptual age of forty-six weeks regardless of their chronological age. However, as the author points out, this only indicates that between a period of forty-two and fifty conceptual weeks, extra exposure to the external environment does not speed up the process. It is the overall period of forty-six weeks from conception that matters.

Environment may be somewhat limited in its effects on the acquisition of early motor behaviours. Dennis' study of the Hopi Indians (Dennis, 1940) gave such an indication. Hopi infants were bound to a cradle board which completely restricted their ability to move their limbs or to move their heads very far. These cradle boards were carried on their mother's backs for the whole of the first three months of the child's life and for a considerable part of each day after that period. Dennis found that these children began to walk at approximately the same time as children who had not been reared in such a restrictive way. It would seem then that the acquisition of the early motor skills depended principally upon the development of the musculature and the neural mechanisms and not upon the infant's ability to practice skills.

Other studies such as that by Gesell and Thompson (1934) tackled the same problem by attempting to prematurely enrich the environment of individuals. In this case one of a pair of identical twins was encouraged to acquire the art of climbing stairs at the age of forty-six weeks and intensive practice was given until the child could climb the stairs with considerable skill. At this point the other twin was introduced to the climbing task and without practice she was able to climb the stairs without too much difficulty and in a period of two weeks had equalled and even surpassed that of her twin sister. The authors concluded that the appearance of this motor skill was primarily dependent upon the ripening of neural structures in the infant and was little affected by practice and exercise.

Evidence from other studies suggest that this is not always the case, however. Whilst it would seem that the onset of certain behaviours may very often be dependent upon maturation, it also seems that if the onset of the behaviours is to result in successful accomplishment of later skills then an input from the environment is necessary. As an example of this, studies of the babbling behaviour of infants suggest that this occurs spontaneously. Both hearing and deaf infants commence babbling at approximately the same time, at a chronological age of about five months. Both sets of infants will continue to babble for the same length of time. Towards the end of the first year of life the hearing infants begin to transform their random babbling into spoken language. At this stage feedback from the environment is essential. For the deaf children the babbling will gradually disappear. Bower concludes:

> we must agree that the learning theorists are wrong in asserting that behaviour will remain stationary in the absence of environmental stimulation. Behaviour as we have seen will change regardless; but the change need not be successful. In the absence of relevent input from the environment, behaviour may take a completely aberrant direction, that direction may become so firmly established no environmental intervention will suffice to redirect the behaviour back to its proper course.

Rates of Growth and Development

Because a child's development is dependent upon the complex interaction of genetic and environmental factors its chronological age may give little indication of its capabilities, and it has become customary to refer to a child's *developmental age*. This concept is considered a more satisfactory way of describing the level of growth and development which may not be entirely consonant with chronological age. For the young child developmental age is often ascertained by checking his motor accomplishments against an inventory, such as that produced by Sheridan (1973). In this context it is important to remember that these tests will give only the *norm* for a given age range, i.e. the performance that can be expected of the average child as tested on trials. Much confusion can arise from the inappropriate use of such norms as it is important to understand that around each norm is a spread of superior and inferior performances which may still be classified as 'normal' in the sense that they do not indicate that the child is to any significant extent deficient or precocious.

Although the general impression of growth is of a gradual increase in size in all dimensions, closer examination shows that patterns for different systems of the body are quite distinct. In some cases the most rapid development is in the very early stage of life, in others, such as the sex organs, it is just prior to adulthood. Some of these characteristic patterns are illustrated in Figure 2.6. These curves, drawn from Scammon (1930), represent four major types of tissue in the body and the rates at which they develop from birth to maturity. The general

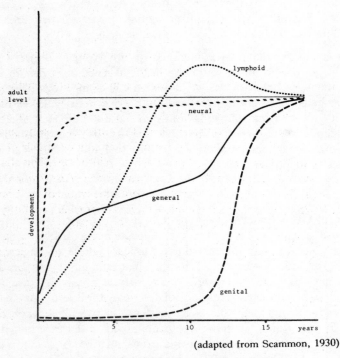

(adapted from Scammon, 1930)

Figure 2.6 Growth curves for various body tissues

tissue represents the bulk of the body as a whole, including weight and external dimensions with the exception of the head and neck which are more closely allied to the neural development related with growth of the brain. The quantity of blood and size of the respiratory and digestive organs also follow this general pattern which shows very rapid rise in volume during early infancy, gradually slowing but with a second acceleration during the pre-adolescent growth spurt. The growth of nerve tissue is most rapid in the first four years and then decelerates rapidly until very little development growth occurs during the later part of childhood. This trend is quite different from that of genital growth, the development of the sex organs occurring almost exclusively during the period of puberty from the age of twelve years onwards. A curve for lymphoid tissue is the most atypical. The lymph glands constitute an internal protective mechanism against infection and the bulk of these including the adenoids, tonsils and thymus gland is at the greatest as a proportion of the total body bulk from the ages of ten to twelve and then diminishes. In particular the thymus gland in the chest atrophies and almost disappears in the adult body.

The comparison of developmental age with chronological age has already been made. It was indicated that in early childhood the customary way of ascertaining developmental age is by means of a developmental schedule. There is however a more accurate method of doing this which uses the gradual changes which occur in the skeleton. At birth very little of the human skeleton is in the form of bone as we customarily think of it; rather it is in the form of a soft, pliable cartilaginous substance. Over the period of childhood much of this substance will gradually ossify, that is it will turn into bone. This change occurs at various sites on the bones known as *centres of ossification*, and gradually spreads out from those centres until the whole of the bone is ossified. When this process is complete there is no further capability for increase in stature. By X-ray examination of a skeleton of a child it is possible to determine the extent to which this process of ossification has taken place. A child who appears to be very large for his age may, on examination of X-ray pictures, be shown to have an almost completely ossified skeleton. Thus he is simply an early developer and is unlikely to develop much further. However, a large child whose level of ossification was still relatively low would have capability for considerable growth and may develop into an exceptionally large adult.

The period of childhood ends with the onset of puberty when the reproductive organs achieve maturity. This usually occurs at the age of about twelve in girls and fourteen in boys, but there are wide variations. The pre-pubertal growth spurt begins two years before the actual onset of sexual fertility; the latter being signified by the onset of the menstrual cycle in girls and by capacity for ejaculation in boys. Though as the latter is very difficult to determine accurately the presence of pigmented pubic hair is often taken as its equivalent. The physical changes at puberty are stimulated by the secretion of hormones into the blood-stream from the ovaries or testes and the adrenal glands. These have the effects of developing not only the primary sexual characteristics, that is the enlargement of the breasts and uterus in the female and the enlargement of the penis in the male, but also of the secondary sexual characteristics; the development of the muscular neck and wider shoulders in the male and of the wider hips in the female and the growth of coarse pigmented hair on the body. Whilst this physical metamor-phosis is extremely important in itself it is noteworthy that such changes cannot take place without concomitant psychological changes. The way the individual will react to peers and to the rest of society may be profoundly influenced by changes that occur in physique and physical capabilities. The total phenomenon is referred to as *adolescence*, the physical manifestation as *puberty*, and the onset of menstruation in the female as *menarche*.

The age at which puberty occurs can differ widely within a given population. It is not uncommon in Great Britain to find girls of ten approaching puberty and other girls of thirteen and fourteen who are not yet sexually mature. This variation is normal and an equivalent variation occurs in boys some two years after the girls. Tanner (1962) indicated that there was evidence that the age at which puberty occured was decreasing at a quite remarkable level (a phenomenon known as the *secular trend*). His studies were hampered by the absence of reliable evidence and historical records in many countries, but nevertheless he was able to conclude with a reasonable degree of certainty that over the past century such a trend had been very clearly demonstrated. Whilst changes in a species are to be expected, the rate of this trend (three months in every ten years) was remarkable.

Explanations of why the age of puberty should have continued to decrease for such a period of time are not very convincing. Tanner examined a number of these and found them unsatisfactory. One such explanation suggested that 'normal' age of puberty was considerably earlier than that which had been witnessed in the nineteenth century. The delay was thought to be the effect of poor environmental conditions operative during the industrial revolution. The gradual improvement in these conditions meant that this 'normal' trend was now being achieved again. Evidence from children of upper middle class families during the last century led Tanner to suppose that this explanation was unacceptable. Although these people would have suffered no hardship, indeed they may well have had superior environmental conditions at that time, the same trend was present in their records. There is a similar trend indicated in the countries which have not undergone an industrial revolution – further evidence that this explanation is unsatisfactory.

The argument that the increasingly early age of puberty is a genetic pattern of mankind is equally unacceptable. Extrapolation of the trends readily shows it would require mankind to have reached sexual fertility at very late years in his early history and would indicate that in years to come that fertility might be achieved during early infancy. Such conjecture seems absurd.

A more plausible explanation takes into account technical advances which have given man increased mobility. If a social group is relatively isolated, and marriage partners are, of necessity, drawn from the same group, the balance of genes available is relatively static. That is, the proportion of any particular type of gene in the *gene pool* remains the same and the characteristics of the population remain roughly the same. A sudden change, brought about by intermarriage with people from another gene pool, could change this. Widespread human mobility has only recently occurred.

More recently researchers have been exploring the variations to the average age of puberty which occur within and across cultures. From these more detailed analyses it is clear that there are considerable variations (Tanner and Eveleth, 1974). Taranger (1983) has concluded that the secular trend may well be attributable to a complex interaction of variables such as social class, nutrition, degree of social stimulation, and genetic make-up. These, he suggests, have been improving at different rates in different cultures, and that in some cultures they are approaching an optimum balance and the end of the downward secular trend.

Certainly there is evidence of 'levelling off' in several cultures (Bruntland and Walløe, 1973; Dann and Roberts, 1973), but Tanner's conclusion that the trend was identical in widely different British subcultures does not seem to support the thesis.

The relationship of early and late development to final adult dimensions is one which has received considerable scrutiny. The best evidence available (Tanner, 1970) suggests that the early developer does tend to retain a slight lead on later developers when adult status is achieved, though this difference is not very great. It is interesting that the evidence is contrary to the folk lore belief that late developers will turn out to be much larger than early developers.

Because girls start their pre-adolescent growth some two years before boys the typical schoolgirl in the upper forms of the junior school may be larger and perhaps capable of better athletic performance than many of the boys. This superiority of the average girl from the age of eight to ten rapidly diminishes as more of the boys start their pre-adolescent growth spurts and then becomes reversed as many of the girls reach puberty and cease to grow. By the age of fifteen the average boy will be considerably taller than the average girl and will have concomitantly greater physical strength.

Motor Development

The infant can demonstrate a large number of motor capacities. In the past it has been customary to subdivide these into *reflexes*, which are automatic, unlearned responses to stimulation, and responses involving maturation and learning. More recently this tidy dichotomy has been somewhat confused by a growing body of research indicating the existence of certain behaviours, hitherto considered the products of learning, at ages when such learning seems unlikely to have occurred. However, for the sake of clarity, we shall consider first the conventional views and then the new evidence.

The first year is begun with a repertoire of reflex actions. Some of these, such as swallowing, turning to avoid irritation, sucking, coughing etc., have vital roles to play in the survival of the infant. This is not to say that they will not be subject to modification by later learning, but in the relatively helpless stages of infancy they function in quite limited and stereotyped ways.

In addition there are reflexes which appear to serve little purpose. The new-born child has a surprisingly strong grip, sufficient for it to support its whole body weight; and the toes, though too short to be functional, will also curl around a finger or pencil as though to grip it. The 'startle' response to noise or sudden movement consists of the sudden extension of arms and legs and throwing back of the head with such force that often the trunk is lifted momentarily from the surface on which the infant is lying. These, and similar reflexes, rapidly disappear during the first few months of life. We can only speculate as to their origins. A strong grip is certainly a prerequisite for many species of ape and monkey, which carry their young clinging to the mother's hair. Perhaps at some time our ancestors behaved in similar fashion. Similarly one could suggest that an unattended infant might, by sudden, violent movements, manage to delay the attentions of a predator until vital help arrived. Yet other reflexes are not so easily interpreted, such as the primary 'walking' reflex displayed when a newborn infant is held with its feet touching the ground. Even if encouraged to practise the infant will lose this behaviour within a few months.

Highly detailed schedules of the emergence of crawling, sitting and similar motor activities have been produced (Gesell, Thompson and Amatruda, 1934). These illustrate the progression from rudimentary limb movements to sophisticated behaviours. Such schedules are often broken down into stages, although the actual behavioural sequences shows a gradual transition from start to finish. Therefore a 'stage' is not really a discrete type of behaviour, but a prominent characteristic of a phase of the developing activity. For example, an infant may reach the stage of creeping on hands and knees at forty weeks; but it would be difficult to determine the exact day on which this behaviour occurred. Rather, there would be a gradual differentiation from crawling on the stomach, to crawling on the hands and knees, to progressing on hands and feet, over a period of some twenty weeks commencing at about week thirty. It has already been observed that the ages at which behaviours occur show wide variation within the normal population. Authorities agree that, whilst this is so, the progression from stage to stage tends to be invariant. Some infants may remain in a stage for a considerable time whilst others pass through two or three quite quickly, although this may not be apparent to the casual observer.

It was observed earlier (Dennis, 1940) that maturation plays a very important part in the development of many motor skills. Reference has also been made to recent analyses by Bower (1973) which indicate that reaching behaviour shows some intriguing changes. The young infant will both reach and grasp for an object with a co-ordinated movement which seems quite sophisticated in terms of accommodation to size and distance of the object. However, over a period of time the reaching will persist but the grasping will disappear, a phenomenon which might appear as a regression. The author suggests that the grasping of an observed object (often a dangling toy) is seldom successful and so the child ceases to employ it. He will not stop grasping his toys or blankets in the pram because in that situation the grasp is associated with tactile stimulation, and, as the objects are stationary, the grasp is successful. The reaching component is successful, often leading to interesting movements of objects even if they are not secured, so this will remain. Grasping occurs in older infants after the object has been touched. Further investigations of children from six to nine months indicated that there were changes in the strength of grip for objects of different weights, at first after the object was in the hand, and subsequently by adjustment to previous experience of the same object. Bower's arguments extend far beyond the simple descriptive schedules of earlier studies. It is clear that his interpretations place us in a position in which we cannot consider motor development as separate from intellectual development. The necessity to relinquish a fairly successful but unvarying reach and grasp suggests an increasingly sophisticated way of construing the environment.

The second year usually begins with the average child having achieved the ability to stand and to walk if supported. Within another two to three months he will walk unaided. Again, there are wide variations within the normal population and the observer may expect to find children of ten or eleven months making their first unsupported steps, whilst others may stick firmly on all-fours until they are almost two years old.

Standard inventories indicate an increasing wealth of motor accomplishments which maturation of the nerve and muscle systems on the one hand, and extended opportunities for learning on the other hand, will produce. The two-year--old can usually throw a ball, pull a truck, manipulate a pencil or brush, stand objects upon one another or within one another and many similar activites. Many of the motor skills which cannot yet be performed do not require basic behaviours of a different kind, but require more sophisticated co-ordination and in some cases increases in strength. For instance, we would not expect a two-year-old to be able to produce a reasonable copy of a circle with pencil and paper, yet he possesses all the basic accomplishments. He can hold a pencil firmly, move his arm and hand in any given direction and can easily distinguish a circle from other geometrical shapes. What he cannot do is fit these abilities together into the necessary sequence.

From the third year onward the development of motor skills progresses steadily. Clearly the influence of changes in the child's intellectual capacities (Chapters 3 and 4) will have a considerable bearing on the level of motor skills, as will increases in strength and stature.

3

Perceptual Development

What is Perception?

To each person the reality of perceiving something is undeniable. As the reader looks at this page he is aware of a white sheet with black markings upon it. Unfortunately the quality of the 'whiteness' he experiences is not open to investigation. Only observable responses such as 'that page is white' are available, and these may accompany or follow the internal events, but they are not part of them. Some aspects of the preceding events are well documented. Perceiving may involve any of the senses, and physical stimulation of the nervous system by the external environment is quite well understood.

The various sense organs in the eyes, ears, nose, tongue and skin consist of specialised cells which respond to particular forms of stimulation. Cells in the retina of the eye respond to specific electromagnetic wavelengths within the visible spectrum and produce appropriate electrical impulses for transmission to the brain. The type of cell activated will depend upon the wavelength, and the site of the cell will denote the position of the source relative to the eyeball. Taste and odour sensations are produced by chemical activity upon the taste buds in the tongue and olfactory receptors in the nasal cavity respectively. Compression waves in the air cause vibrations in the tympanic membranes of the ears which are then transmitted through small bones, or ossicles, to the receptors in the inner ear. The skin is furnished with a vast array of highly specialised receptors just below the surface. Different cells will react to different features of the stimulus, such as temperature and pressure. Each of these systems has the function of transforming the stimulation it receives into an electrical charge which can be transmitted through the body's nerves. Because each cell responds to a different form of stimulation the messages are to some extent *analysed* as well as transmitted.

There are other sensory mechanisms which operate within the body, carrying messages relating to its internal environment e.g. pain receptors in the gut and other receptors which relay messages concerning the body's internal environment and its relationship to the external environment. Of the latter the hemispherical canals of the inner ear are perhaps the best known. These canals contain small calcareous balls which change location as the body moves. By means of these the brain is able to obtain continuous feedback on its position relative to the ground, enabling the body to be adjusted to maintain balance.

When receptor cells in the body respond to stimulation they produce an electrical voltage change which is passed down the nerve pathways to the brain. Nerves transmit this voltage on what is called an *all or none principle*. That is, if the voltage is sufficiently large to overcome the resistance of the nerve cell (its limen) it will transmit. If not, nothing will happen. More intense sensations of a louder noise or a brighter light can only be signalled by the number of pathways which transmit simultaneously. Once the limen is overcome a single cell simply transmits or 'fires'. Stimuli are said to be *subliminal* if they do not 'fire' the nerve cells, and hence the conscious brain is not aware of them.

Yet perception must involve more than these biological processes of sensation. When the impulses have reached the brain they must be identified, and if they are to be useful they must be interpreted. Thus, looking at the white page, the brain must analyse the pattern of impulses to discover what sort of stimulus is before the eyes. Having analysed them, it must then try to match with previous images stored in memory. If this is successful the reader will recognise the white page, though he does not need to have verbal labels unless he wishes someone else to know that he's recognised it as such.

The separation of perceptual development from cognitive development (Chapter 4) is an arbitrary decision. Whilst it may aid the reader (and the author) to take these aspects of development one at a time, in another respect it is counterproductive. Only one feature is totally distinctive, and that is the sensory input which initiates perception. Thereafter perception and cognition become inextricably mixed. The fact that the flickering flames of a fire produce light waves which impinge upon the eye of the child is no guarantee that the child will perceive the fire; that is, that he will be able to identify the sensory input as something meaningful. In order to do that he may have to categorise the input within some matrix of images, maybe the word 'fire' spoken by a parent, maybe other flickering objects such as daddy's

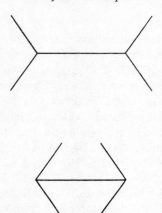

Figure 3.1 The Müller-Lyer Illusion

cigarette lighter, the gas cooker etc. The first few exposures may produce little in the way of perception and it could take some time before the sensory data can be rapidly identified and classified in the child's store of information. Authorities do not agree on this however.

The *nativist* tradition believes that some of these processes are inherited. Founders of the *Gestalt* school of psychology took the view that the brain automatically built up patterns of stimuli so that a complete form was perceived. Much of their work made use of visual illusions such as the Müller-Lyer Illusion (Figure 3.1). The fact that people perceive the equal horizontal lines to be of different lengths, was, they argued, evidence that they were influenced by the whole configuration (or gestalt), rather than by a pattern which was built up of perceptions of individual lines. Similarly, when a person hears a melody it does not become unrecognisable if the key is transposed, although each element is now quite different. The evidence that people's perceptions are heavily biased toward configurations is very strong. What is more problematic is the assertion that the processes which achieve these configurations are innate.

Contrary views are held by the empiricists who argue that the sensory stimulation can only produce perception when the infant has stored certain data. According to their views the earliest sensory events must be totally meaningless, and only through learning processes can the child begin to analyse the input and begin to form coherent perceptions of events. The following two sections contain evidence relating to this problem.

Perceptual Constancy

Perceptual mechanisms enable the individual to recognise stimuli which have been experienced before, even if he now experiences them in a rather different way. Puzzle photographs in which everyday objects such as a pair of scissors or a toothbrush are viewed from an odd angle and in very fine detail, test this capacity to its limit. In day-to-day experience this capacity is used too. Aerial photographs of familiar places, the sight of a neighbour's child up a tree, or the rapidly changing image of a coin spinning, do not lead us to change our knowledge of how these things are constructed. Similarly a car we know to be red remains red, whether we see it at dusk, in bright sunlight or under artificial lighting. We have no difficulty in accepting these into a perception of a world which is stable and predictable.

If an infant is to operate efficiently in his environment he too must recognise that there are certain features of it which are constant, though sense impressions may suggest otherwise. When mother walks away, he should not fear that she is diminishing in stature, even though the image on his retina is diminishing. Similarly he will need to recognise a yellow teddy bear, even though in bright daylight it is golden yellow, and in the dimly lit bedroom it may appear greyish-brown. Failure to perceive these constancies would leave him with little competence in a world with irregular fluctuations and changes.

The weight of evidence suggests that learning is the process by which this is achieved. Indeed much of Piaget's theory of cognitive develop-

(adapted from Gibson, 1960)

Figure 3.2 The 'visual cliff'

ment (Chapter 4) is about this process, and has been succinctly summarised as denoting a gradual emancipation from perception.

The young infant responds to certain constancies very quickly, however. It should not be thought that the nativist theory is without foundation. The well-known visual cliff experiment (Gibson and Walk, 1960) indicated that during the first year of life many infants refused to move over what appeared to be a drop of more than three feet, even though encouraged to do so by their mothers. The apparatus is illustrated in Figure 3.2.

The chequer board patterning on both sides of the screen enabled any child with depth perception to determine that there was a drop, although the glass plate would have prevented him from actually falling. This is not outright endorsement for a nativist viewpoint, of course. Increasingly we are being presented with findings which suggest that a great deal is happening in those first six months and this evidence does not tell us whether the child has already learned about depth perception or whether he has an innate ability to perceive depth.

Whilst most theorists have tended to favour an empiricist interpretation, current research into the abilities of the neonate, or new-born child, are suggesting several competencies at very early ages and it may be necessary to reevaluate the position in the not-too-distant future. With reference to the problem of size constancy at different distances, mentioned earlier, Bower (1974) has shown that the defensive posture adopted by infants of only a few weeks is dependent upon an ability to infer the distance of an object from the face. When exposing a small object and moving it close to the face of a neonate the defensive reaction was seen. When a larger object was placed at a greater distance and then moved to a closer position so that the image on the retina remained the same no reaction was seen (Figure 3.3). This suggests that very young infants have the capacity to estimate distances in a very complex way, using binocular vision. If such a capacity has been learned, the process must have been accomplished most efficiently, and presumably from few exposures to stimuli. This is not a necessary inference, however. The reaction could be a form of reflex action triggered off by stimuli of this type, without imputing conscious process.

Perception of Form and Pattern

Fantz (1961) investigated the abilities of infants to perceive differences in the configurations of displays. One problem with the investigations

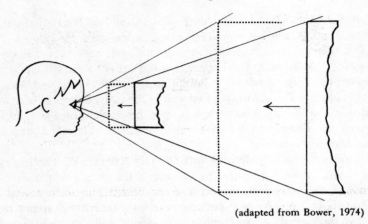

(adapted from Bower, 1974)

Figure 3.3 Same size retinal images projected by objects at different distances

of perception in very young children is the difficulty of finding an appropriate index of their attention or preference. Fantz's method, which is one commonly used, was to measure the precise length of time for which his subjects' eyes fixated upon one of two stimuli presented simultaneously. The pairs of stimuli were varied and were made up of different shapes (squares, circles etc.) painted in patterns or plain colours. His subjects were very young infants of from one week to fifteen weeks of age, and his intention was to determine whether they were able to differentiate between the stimuli sufficiently to show a preference.

In cases where different stimuli were used (e.g. one patterned square, one plain square) the subjects showed marked preference for the more complex. Whilst such experiments are often reported as indicative of 'preference', it would perhaps be safer to describe them as indicative of attention span. As Wohlwill (1968) points out, a more complex stimulus demands longer scrutiny, before any preference decision may be appropriate.

Even if the infants were not genuinely 'preferring' the complex patterns, it seems highly probable that they were discriminating between the stimuli presented. On that basis Fantz developed another experiment (Fantz *et al*, 1962) using stimuli consisting of black and white stripes of various widths in comparison with plain grey cards. He predicted that if the infant was unable to resolve the stripes they would appear as a grey card and no preference would be shown. It was

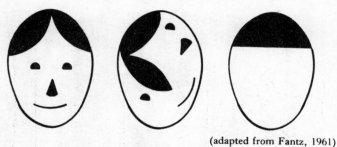

(adapted from Fantz, 1961)

Figure 3.4 'Scrambled faces' used in infant perception experiments

observed that infants of less than four weeks could distinguish one-eight inch stripes from plain grey and up to one-sixty-fourth inch stripes by six months.

Fantz concluded that whilst visual acuity increased substantially during the first six months of life, some patterned vision exists in the new-born child.

In a subsequent experiment Fantz (1963) investigated the abilities of five day old infants to distinguish certain common configurations of patterns, such as the human face, from stimuli containing the same pattern elements but in scrambled form. His results indicated that very young infants spent much longer looking at the realistic face than at the scrambled one; and that they paid little attention to any of the control patterns (Figure 3.4). The author emphasised that his results did not imply an innate recognition of the human face, but that a pattern with close similarities to social objects had marked stimulus properties. This could have important implications for later development of social interaction.

Other researchers have emphasised the importance of active involvement in the development of perceptual abilities. An interesting example of research in this field is that of Held and Hein (1963). Kittens were raised in the dark for ten weeks, resulting in retarded perceptual development. They did not respond to the visual cliff experiment, straying over to the 'dangerous' side. Pairs of kittens were then placed on a 'carousel' in a circular compartment (Figure 3.5). Both could see the same patterned walls of this compartment but one was contained so that it was moved only by the activity of the other. After thirty hours exposure all the active kittens chose the 'safe' side of the visual cliff; but the passive kittens continued to behave randomly. This suggests that normal perceptual development may involve complex interactions with

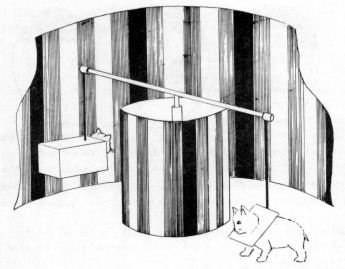

(adapted from Held and Hein, 1963)

Figure 3.5 Active and passive visual stimulation

learning in other areas, and that active involvement in the learning process is an important prerequisite.

By rearing new-born kittens with translucent eye-covers for two months Hubel and Wiesel (1963) showed that the innate mechanisms in the visual apparatus which detected sloping lines ceased to function. Clearly diffuse light was inadequate stimulation for the maintenance of the mechanisms, but it is not known how much normal experience is needed to maintain them. Presumably it is minimal.

Developments in eye surgery have presented researchers with some rather similar instances in humans. A considerable number of reports have been published of patients who have been given sight in adulthood by the removal of congenital cataracts (von Senden, 1932). Taken at face value the studies suggest that these patients are unable to integrate their newly acquired visual faculty into their other sense perceptions without considerable effort and a period of learning. In one case a woman had been made thoroughly familiar with some solid blocks, and she was able to identify them by touch as cones, spheres, cylinders etc. When her sight was restored she was for some time not able to identify them without first touching them.

Unfortunately these early studies are anecdotal and have been heavily criticised. It had been assumed that, because cataracts let diffuse light through onto the retina no deterioration would have occurred. Hubel and Wiesel's study must now cast doubt upon that supposition. On the other hand von Senden's reports do suggest that eventually the patients were able to perceive visually. If one interprets Hubel and Wiesel's study as showing degeneration of the retina this should not be possible.

The anecdotal reports were seen as casting grave doubt upon the Gestaltist notions of innate mechanisms for synthesising sensory inputs. Their theory would have predicted an immediate assimilation of the new sensory information into the existing pattern of perception.

Attention and Perception

If we reflect upon the position of a young child in the home or in the school, or if we think of our own situation, it will be apparent that there are very many stimuli which are sufficiently intense to be perceived. Yet for most of the time we do not perceive them. As I write this I can hear the noise of passing traffic and the sound of rain on the roof, but a few seconds before I did not perceive them. In everyday parlance I heard them when I had drawn attention to them.

Attention has been compared to a filter process, and to a tuning process like that on a radio receiver. Initially it was thought that certain physical properties, such as the intensity of the stimuli, commanded attention. More specifically it was found that the human senses respond to *changes* in stimulation. Even very intense stimuli such as loud noises can be filtered out if they are continuous or occur at regular intervals; but variations in intensity or the interval tend to attract attention. Similarly the flickering of the eyeball serves to change the position of an image on the retina. If lenses are fitted which maintain the position of the image in one spot, the image will cease to be perceived. This phenomenon is known as *habituation*.

More recently emphasis has been upon the meaningfulness of a stimulus. In this interpretation expectations, based upon previous experience, permit selective attention. Melzack (1965) has argued that, as the infant will not have many stored experiences, his perceptual processes may be over-loaded by massive sensory input. However, this view is highly contentious and, as we shall see, others believe the new-born infant to be equipped with certain attentional mechanisms.

Lewis and Goldberg (1969) found that children of three years of age paid less attention to familiar stimuli after novel stimuli had been introduced. Their estimates of attention were eye fixation (as utilised by Fantz) and heart-rate, smiling responses and pointing gestures. They argued that novel stimuli increased the infant's state of uncertainty, making them less attentive to the original familiar stimuli.

Perception As a Continuing Process

It is likely that there are some quantitative and qualitative differences in the extent to which young infants and older children and adults are presented with situations in which there are novel stimuli to be perceived. Whilst we would not want to endorse James' (1890) view that the infant's world is a 'buzzing, blooming confusion', it would be reasonable to say that the infant is frequently presented with stimulation which is novel, that is, which is not readily related to experiences already in his memory store. As the child gets older this will obviously become less so. Indeed it seems likely that the older child or adult will also develop strategies to deal with unknown stimuli as quickly and efficiently as possible. One might compare this to a situation in which a young child, unable to read or speak, and with little experience, is placed in a strange town without assistance. He would probably be at the mercy of whatever circumstances befell him. Whereas if an adult were placed in the middle of a strange town in some unfamiliar foreign country, he would not be able to ask directly for help, but there would be sufficient similarities with familiar environments to give direction to his investigations. He would know which buildings could be hotels, shops etc. and would be able to secure some form of transportation given sufficient time and ingenuity. He might make some amusing or embarrassing mistakes but it is unlikely that he would be unable to survive.

It would seem, therefore, that it is now more pertinent to look at these intellectual processes which are used in interpreting the sensory data.

Neisser (1967) considered the problem of pattern recognition. He was attempting to define the limits of distortion within which we can still recognise a hand-written letter *A*. Figure 3.6 is similar to the enlarged photographs of recognisable hand-printed letters which he presented (Neisser and Weene, 1960). He was concerned to identify the nature of the 'recognition' process which identified them as members of a

(similar to letters used by Neisser and Weene, 1960)

Figure 3.6 Recognisable forms of hand-written letter 'A'

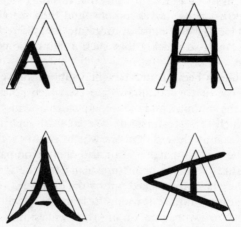

Figure 3.7 Mismatch of stimuli and simple template

category, even though there were quite discernible variations between them.

One form of explanation he termed *template-matching*. This theory suggested that there is a stored image of a basic model, and that each new stimulus was checked against it. There are obvious problems to this sort of interpretation. If the template is thought of as a memory structure it would have to be localised, and would then fail to recognise many quite acceptable letters simply because they were different in size or orientation, or because they impinged upon a different portion of the retina (Figure 3.7). It is possible to argue that each individual stimulus will provide a template, so that eventually the child will have acquired a 'retina full' of templates for the letter *A* in various sizes and various positions. This does not seem to be the case however, as subjects are able to recognise an object after having seen it only once before, and in conditions which ensure that a different portion of the retina is stimulated on the second occasion. There is the added problem that multiple templates would place an excessive load upon the memory of the individual.

To some extent these reservations can be met by modifying the template theory so that the template becomes a composite of the previously recognised stimuli. By this means the memory strain could be greatly reduced. The process of identification can then be compared to that of sorting through the attributes in an Identikit in order to match a stored memory of a face. It seems that this may sometimes happen, when we experience a novel stimulus and then search round in our memory store for the most appropriate identifier, but usually we recognise stimuli so quickly that such a cumbersome system seems implausible.

A more likely theory is that the child subjects his sensations to two processes. The first is a scanning process which notes the distinctive features of the stimulus, and the second which attends to the particular ways in which these features are related. Although this may sound laborious it is much less so than one which requires sorting through an array for the nearest match. It can also operate on partial data. Very brief exposure of words or pictures can often be identified if some salient feature has been picked out by the observer. This can often be seen in children who are learning to read. They will pick out some characteristic of a word ('oo' or 'ing') and will estimate its nature from this.

As the infant grows older he learns to pay attention to other characteristics of the stimulus, thereby improving his recognition. Whilst recent evidence suggests that the new-born infant can distinguish distance, shape and pattern, perceptual mechanisms are not immutable. When children aged four to eight years were asked to select abstract symbols which matched a stimulus symbol, an age difference was found on only one dimension, orientation (Gibson, Gibson, Pick and Osser, 1962). The younger children were uninfluenced by the orientation of the symbol and reported it as matching the stimulus even when it was inclined at 45° to the vertical. Older children made few such errors. Thus it would seem that at some stage between the ages of four to eight

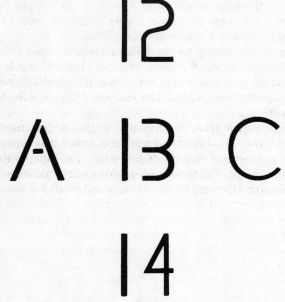

Figure 3.8 Context and stimulus meaning

years orientation becomes a salient feature of perception.

From evidence of this sort (see Bryant, 1971) it seems that the development of a perceptual ability consists of a series of re-orientations of the inborn capacity, enabling the individual to assimilate further attributes of the stimulus.

With respect to reading skills, one such development involves the use of context. As the child's experiences increase he begins to anticipate the type of stimulus which will arrive, so that the area of search for identification is narrowed down. Figure 3.8 is a good example of an ambiguous figure embedded in two different contexts. Most people have no difficulty in identifying the central item as either a *B* or a *13*, depending on which they expected to see in that context.

There is also compelling evidence that the extent to which an array of stimuli can be perceived, understood, and remembered is very much influenced by familiarity, i.e. previous learning. Learning the highly specialised skills of playing chess can be started at a very early age. If an interim point in a game is exposed to view for a brief period of about 5 seconds, young chess players are able to recall and reproduce much more of it than can adults who have little or no playing ability. However, if the chess pieces are placed randomly on the board this superiority disappears (Chase and Chi, 1980).

So the child's ability to recognise a stimulus may involve some inherent competencies, but there is good evidence that it is largely dependent upon his ability to identify the sensation and classify it in the light of previous experiences. The reaction of the nervous system to stimulation is not that of a passive recording device. Perception involves extracting patterns from the input and linking them with existing knowledge. It is a process of construction rather than recording. It is therefore appropriate that we should now look more closely at the intellectual processes which are developing and the growth of the store of information which the child can utilise in his transactions with the environment.

4

Cognitive Development

What are Concepts?

People behave in ways which suggest that they perceive similarities between objects or events in their environment. It does not surprise us if an infant takes an orange and rolls it across the floor as if it is a ball, for we share the concept of *roundness*. Nor are we surprised if the orange has been placed in a bowl with six apples, for it belongs to another shared category, our concept of *edible fruit*. The ability to perceive similarities and to form concepts greatly reduces the strain of living. We do not have to learn anew that an orange will roll, we expect it to roll because it is round like a ball.

Studying concepts is difficult, for we cannot see them, and whilst the older child can tell us that he perceives an orange and a ball as both being round, the infant cannot. Furthermore even adults may use concepts which are not readily expressed in words. Shopping for material for curtains can involve one in elaborate circumlocutions if one tries to define the colour concept one is employing – 'a sort of pinkish, but not bright, more a sort of beige/pink'.

Concepts or roundness, redness, heaviness, etc. are rather simple and may be ascertained by direct sensory experience. Concepts such as energy, familiarity or conservatism, on the other hand, are highly abstract. The popular tune, a neighbour's face and the taste of bacon are all familiar but share no perceptual characteristics. As concepts are not observable we must infer them from the ways people behave.

We may think of a concept as a symbolisation of a group of objects or ideas which an individual classifies as having some common element or elements. Some concepts are shared by nearly all people, such as the concept of *wetness*, whereas others may have idiosyncratic interpretations, such as the concept of *conservatism*. Young children seem to have a concept of 'grown-ups'. They are able to classify people they have

53

never seen before. Of course the classification may not be the same for any two children, and we might be surprised at some of those included in it. A secondary school child might qualify and, sadly, the age of twenty-one may seem the ultimate in senility. This is because the child is strongly influenced by any very clearly perceivable characteristic, in this case height. Throughout childhood height is a fairly good index of age; babies are very small, toddlers are larger, school entrants are larger still. So it is not surprising that the young child adopts height as the discriminating dimension for his concept of 'grown-ups'. In his early years the child is unable to operate this discrimination in conjunction with other criteria such as whether the individual has left school, whether he has children, and so on.

This example suggests another feature of concepts; that they are inter-related. The young child who has classified a neighbouring fifteen-year-old as *grown-up* may also be classifying him as *friend*, neighbour, footballer and *cyclist*. At first such cross-classification can prove perplexing and the child may protest that he cannot be a *neighbour* because he's a *friend*. From this perplexity will develop a highly complex pattern of related concepts.

Concept Formation

In a fascinating and detailed study of the use of verbal labels for objects in the environment, Lewis (1951) showed how a young child *expanded* and *contracted* the meaning of words. By this he meant that the child would use a word (or his personal form of the word) to denote an object, and would then use that label for other similar objects for a time. Later new words would be introduced to separate the identities. The meaning of one of the words had then been contracted (Figure 4.1). At an early stage *tee* is used to denote a cat. It is then expanded to denote other animals such as a horse. Later the utility of this expanded meaning disappears and a new word *hosh* appears to denote a horse.

We cannot be sure that the changing usage of words was indicative of changes in the concepts the child was employing. The linguistic phenomena may be relatively unrelated to the underlying structure of concepts, but it is certainly meaningful to suggest that what the words portray is the elaboration of a general, all-purpose, furry, hairy, any-size, animal-type composite concept which provides a temporary means of identifying stimuli. This speedily becomes redundant as the child notes dissimilarities which he needs to take into account. Of course this

age	cat	cow	horse
1;9,11	- - → tee		
1;10,18		- - →tee	
1;11,1			
1;11,24			- - → tee
1;11,25			- - → hosh
1;11,27	pushie		
2;0,20		mooka	

- - →   first use of word
⊥   word no longer used

(adapted from Lewis, 1951)

Figure 4.1 Expansion and contraction of word meanings

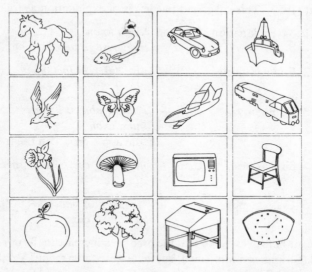

(Brown and others, 1975)

Figure 4.2 Sample of concept cards used by Brown and others

process goes on in a verbal environment and it is unlikely that anything like it would occur if the child was not constantly stimulated by words. Nevertheless concepts do not have to involve verbal expression and, as Furth (1961) and Oléron (1953) have demonstrated, deaf and dumb children do produce quite recognisable forms of concepts although they may be somewhat atypical or retarded.

The use of a *tee* sound for *cat* is not arbitrary. It is most likely a truncated reversal of *cat*. This is described as a common feature of early language, though it has been subject to some re-appraisal by Huttenlocher (1974, see Chapter 5).

An experiment to investigate the use of class concepts by children was conducted in Birmingham (Brown et al, 1969). Class concepts are those which are denoted by class nouns, in this case vehicles) plants, animals and furniture. Sixteen cards with line drawings on them depicted four examples of each of the class concepts (Figure 4.2). These were presented to individual children with the request that they 'put together those which belong'. They were also asked to explain why the cards went together.

The manner in which the children classified the cards was recorded, and their explanations analysed in accordance with a scheme devised by Annett (1959). This suggested five levels of explanation as follows:

Class 1: No explanation   –   '*don't know*',
                                    '*they just go together*', etc.

Class 2: Enumeration   –   *give different fact about each object*

Class 3: Contiguity   –   *relating objects by direct, concrete interaction*
                                    'the apple grows on the tree'

Class 4: Similarities   –   *indicating common characteristics of objects*

Class 5: Class name   –   '*vehicles*' or '*machine*' or '*travel machines*' etc.

The authors discovered that the predicted increase in the use of Class 5 explanations was confirmed, but there were some remarkable features of the trend. The 'no explanations' of Class 1 accounted for 25 per cent of the under-five year olds. This steadily reduced, but even in children of over ten years it did not completely disappear and these oldest

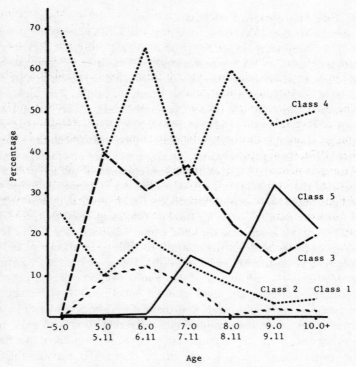

Figure 4.3 Use of five categories of explanation

children were still using more Class 4 explanations than Class 5 (Figure 4.3). It was also found that many children formed more than four groups. Sometimes this was due to what seemed to be a simple lack of appropriate experience, as when some children failed to link mushroom with the other three plants. With the younger children idiosyncratic groupings were often associated with Class 2 explanations however, e.g. 'the clock goes with the T.V. because it tells me the time for Playschool'. Not that there is nothing *wrong* with such answers, but they were often specific to the stimuli and offered little generalisability. If they were evolved from analysing and classifying the perceived objects this is properly termed concept *formation*, but the more 'sophisticated' class concepts were already determined by society and many of the children were in the process of transferring from their personalised concepts to those in common currency. This latter process is more appropriately described as concept *attainment*.

Selecting Appropriate Concepts

Natural phenomena do not automatically fall into conceptual categories. They are placed in them by people because this is the only way in which they can handle the massive input of data from the environment. If we think of any common classification which is in regular use, we can probably find awkward phenomena which do not fit. The biological dichotomy into animal class and vegetable class is very helpful and serves us well for most of the time, but there are some simple organisms which display some of the characteristics of each. Furthermore a single item will exist in many categories. An apple is clearly vegetable, it is also a fruit and a food. Some of these concepts are of higher orders of generality than others (Figure 4.4) and we might enquire whether the child is more likely to acquire its concepts in an upward, downward, or out from the middle direction. Brown (1958) suggested that, whilst it would seem intuitively that the child would begin with a concrete level and move to the abstract (from apple to fruit to food) this would be dependent upon the influence of adults. He postulated a *frequency/ brevity principle* which suggested that adults would be likely to choose (a) the most frequently used concept label, and (b) the shorter expression. This would mean that there would be a tendency in our culture to select the word 'apple' in this hierarchy. It is not longer than the other words and it is in frequent use. The author observed that there were times when this principle broke down. To explain this he introduced a second principle of *equivalence*. This suggested that the parent would introduce a word which was sufficiently, though not too, specific for use in the particular culture. Whereas 'apple' might be satisfactory for a town-dweller, a child on an orchard farm might be

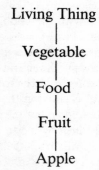

Figure 4.4 Hierarchy of concepts

expected to differentiate between 'windfalls', 'cider apples' and 'dessert apples'. The sub-culture may well have specialised names for these apples.

One is reminded of the tale of an old primary school inspector who visited a rural school in Yorkshire. In the course of a question-and-answer session with a class of seven-year-olds he produced a drawing of a sheep with the query 'Who can tell me what this is?'. Several repeats of the question elicited no answer. In bewilderment the inspector singled out a child and pressed for identification of the animal. Somewhat dubiously the child responded 'appen it's one of Wainwright's blackface, but it's got reight funny 'aunches'.

Language and Conceptualisation

It seems likely that the concepts with which a child structures his view of the world will be closely related to the language he learns. Whether language actually gives him a structure, or whether he structures non-verbally and then labels is a contentious matter. Consider the earlier instance of the child forming a concept of *round*. Initially this concept could be learned by rolling, observing and handling objects, and forming an uncommunicable concept which he later learned to call 'round'. Alternatively, frequent use of the word 'round' by adults may draw to the child's attention the fact that the objects have something in common, their roundness.

Benjamin Whorf proposed that the latter was the case. This view is called the Sapir – Whorf Hypothesis. It suggested that the forms of thinking which were available to people in any culture were dependent upon the language in which they operated. In terms of possible communication between different cultures this was a pessimistic view, as it supposed that the different linguistic forms would be related to different views of the world and to different ways of thinking about it. Thus a child of the Hopi Indian tribe, with no words for future, present and past, would be unable to communicate with, or indeed to think in the same way as, an English child who was familiar with the use of tense.

Much of Whorf's evidence was anecdotal, and empirical studies carried out since that time, whilst supporting the hypothesis suggest that cultural differences may be less profound than was thought. In 1954 Brown and Lenneberg showed that the classification of colours was influenced by the different colour names used in Zuni Indian and American English. Children from the two cultures grouped coloured items into different categories in accordance with the verbal labels available.

Carroll and Casagrande (1958) showed that Navaho Indians use a verb form which indicated the shape of the object in question. The additional cues provided by their language disposed Navaho children to classify objects according to shape whilst English-speaking American children used a colour criterion.

An interesting experiment was conducted by Kelly and Philp (1975) in which they asked children to classify pictures of common objects. All the children were from Papua, New Guinea. They were representative of three groups, two of which attended English-speaking schools and one which did not. One school group was tested in English and the other two groups in Melpa, the vernacular. The authors reported the influence of language upon the classifications of objects as extremely strong, and far in excess of the differences due to school attendance or non-attendance.

An extreme form of the Sapir-Whorf hypothesis is now unacceptable to many authorities. Carroll (1963) has suggested that it be restated in a weaker form. He proposes as an hypothesis that, when languages differ in the ways they encode experience, language users will tend to use categories provided by their language. This will affect their behaviour.

That a language does not have a word for a little-used concept does not necessarily imply that that concept cannot be used. True, it may be used less adroitly than if it were part of common parlance, but that is not quite the same argument. Translators are often presented with situations in which the 'equivalent' word in a second language does not quite give the meaning intended by the originator. The skilful translator will then re-structure a phrase or sentence to maintain *semantic* accuracy.

The Work of L.S. Vygotsky

Vygotsky (1962) conducted an experiment into the ability of children and adults to utilise concepts. His apparatus consisted of twenty-two wooden blocks in five colours, six shapes and with two possible heights and areas of cross-section (see Figure 4.5).

On the base of each block was a nonsense word, each referring to a relationship between height and cross-section, concepts for which the language had no single-word labels. These words were LAG (tall-large), BIK (short-large), MUR (tall-small), and CEV (short-small); the

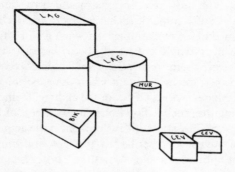

Six of 22 blocks showing two values of height and two values of cross-section.
Blocks are randomly coloured in one of five colours.

Figure 4.5 Sample of Vygotsky's blocks

colours and shapes of the blocks were irrelevant cues. The experimenter
displayed all the blocks before the subject, then picked one, turned it
over to show the label and asked him to pick out those blocks which
'might belong to this kind'. If the subject did not select correctly one of
the wrong blocks would be turned over to show the wrong word and the
experimenter would request that the subject try again. Blocks on which
the label had been revealed were left exposed.

Analysis of the ways in which subjects of different ages tackled this
problem led Vygotsky to the identification of three levels of
sophistication in the formation of a concept. These were described as:

1. *Syncretic conglomerations* (heaps): groups of blocks which were
collected together in a purely random or fortuitous manner, and which
had 'somehow coalesced into an image in his (the subject's) mind ...'

2. *Complexes*: 'objects sited in the child's mind not only by his
subjective impressions but also by bonds actually existing between the
objects'. At this stage the child is clearly classifying in a way which is
intelligible to the observer, although the system still contains idiosyn-
crasies and inconsistencies.

Complexes are subdivided into various categories such as *serial
grouping*, in which each block is linked to the one preceding it (small
blue cylinder – large red cylinder – small red rectangle – small green
cylinder); or *matching to a nuclear block* (collecting all those with any
similarity to the first stimulus block).

Also in this category Vygotsky included *pseudo-concepts*. These would appear to be ordinary concepts in which the subject grouped together all blocks with some clear characteristic and declared that they were of the same kind. For example if shown a green cylinder with the word CEV on it he would collect all the cylinders (or all the green blocks) and declare them to be all CEVs. The nature of the pseudo-concept is shown to be inconsistent when the experimenter indicates that one of the blocks is not a CEV, for the child will remove that block without realising that such action invalidates the rest of his grouping.

3. *Concepts*: the final stage of development is the acquisition of true concepts, which Vygotsky described as 'resilient, uniform, and abstract in nature'. Not until adolescence were these concepts evinced.

This experiment is often cited as one of the most significant in the area of conceptualisation. However, it is not without its critics and some of the criticisms (particularly those raised by Fodor, 1972) are worth close scrutiny.

In the first place the experiment is not really concerned with concept *formation* as Vygotsky claimed, but with concept attainment, for the relevant criteria for success had already been determined in advance of the experiment. The child is being asked to operate in terms of a few properties, colour, size and shape, but to ignore weight, texture or position which could be equally useful. Additionally Fodor argues that the use of a new word does not indicate that the process is one of concept formation but that it is one of concept attainment with an additional translation task (e.g. BIK = 'short' and 'wide').

Second, Vygotsky claims that there is a progression to levels of higher abstraction, yet many adult concepts have no sensory attributes to start with. For example, what are the observably common features of 'furniture' or 'family'? Yet children acquire these concepts adequately. If it is claimed that the invariants are, in these cases, not of *form* but of *function*, the case is still weakened, for function is a very abstract concept with which to begin. Fodor also suggests that criteria such as 'all the ones I like', one of the 'over-abundance of subjective connections' which make up the reasons for the formation of heaps, is neither less abstract, less sensible nor less sophisticated that 'all those that are blue and square'.

Fodor argues that, whilst there may well be differences between the behaviours of children and adults on this task, there is little evidence that they are caused by anything other than the ways in which people perceive the tasks. This is an important criticism. It has been discussed at length because Vygotsky's experiment typifies a host of experiments which purport to establish different conceptual processes in the child. We have already seen (Chapter 3) that perceptual abilities are developmentally organised. If Fodor's criticisms are justified, the levels of concept formation indicated by performance with Vygotsky's blocks may be differences in perception rather than fundamental differences in the ways concepts are formed.

The Work of J.S. Bruner

There have been many other experiments into concept formation and concept attainment, notable amongst which have been those of Bruner and his co-workers (Bruner et al, 1956). These have been concerned with the *strategies* employed by individuals when attempting to achieve concepts in problem-solving situations.

Bruner's thesis was that the study of children in problem-solving situations had concentrated too much upon the nature of the tasks and the stimuli presented to the child, and too little upon the dynamic qualities the child brought to the tasks in order to solve them. One important aspect of the development of strategies would be the gradual progression from reliance upon the immediate and obvious representations of the stimuli (e.g. how they *appeared*) to representations which used symbols or words and which were capable of greater generalisation. Such techniques were described as being of a 'higher order ... for processing information by consecutive inferential steps that takes one beyond what can be pointed at' (Bruner, 1964). The simpler forms of representation of an object in the child's mind are by *enactive* or *iconic* means. The former occurs when the image of an object is constituted of certain characteristics of that object inextricably combined with certain motor aspects of the child's behaviour. In describing this form of representation, Bruner used evidence cited by Piaget (1954) that the very young child is not aware of the extent of his body boundaries and the 'otherness' of things beyond it. A baby shaking a rattle will tend to shake the arm harder if the rattle is dropped, as though in an attempt to regain the noise. The concept of rattle is represented by the physical sensations of rattling. Such behaviour has serious limitations because the child cannot generalise the concept to think about rattles in general, or to consider other people's rattles. He can only represent that one upon which he acts. Other forms of enactive representation will stay with the individual throughout life. Most people agree that learning to play tennis, or golf, or to ride a bicycle, require one to 'get the feel' of the activity. The best textbook available does not seem to accomplish the same end, the representation is inextricably bound up with the bodily 'feel' of the concept.

Subsequently the child develops another form of representation using images. This is known as *iconic* representation, in which a mental picture of an object can be used as a substitute for the object itself. The ability to form iconic images constitutes a very substantial advance in mental functioning. By forming an image the child can think about objects which are not actually present. It is also a limited system however, because icons are formed from the perceptions of prominent, 'knowable' characteristics of an object, such as its shape, colour, smell, etc. So although the child does not have to be actively engaged in motor involvement with an object, he does have to be able to perceive clear sensory attributes of it. Presumably icons of *my teddy bear* and *Mummy* are readily formed, but *motherhood* or *happiness* would be inadequately represented.

The third and most sophisticated form or representation is known as *symbolic* representation. Symbols differ from icons in that the former are purely arbitrary in nature. A photograph or a model of a cow would be an icon in that it would represent the animal in a very real and obvious way. The symbols C-O-W have no such characteristics, they only signify the existence of the animal by concensus of those who use the word. By eliminating the idiosyncracies or special characteristics which an icon portrays (for it will have to represent *a* cow) the symbol enables us to work with a general concept unconstrained by particulars. Whilst there are some marked differences between the views of Bruner and Piaget, it should be clear that this progression could well be summarised by that phrase already used to introduce Piagetian theory, 'emancipation from perception'.

An experiment conducted by one of Bruner's associates (Olson, 1966) used a board holding five rows of seven red light bulbs which could be masked down to three by three or five by five. Switches at the rear enabled the experimenter to connect the bulbs to produce any particular pattern of lights he chose. The rear switches over-rode those on the front control which were used by the subject, so that if the rear switches were all 'off' except for the top row, the child was only able to illuminate the top row. (Figure 4.6). The configuration of the front switches copied that of the display lights.

One, two or more diagrams were then presented, each showing a possible configuration of the lights, and the child was asked to

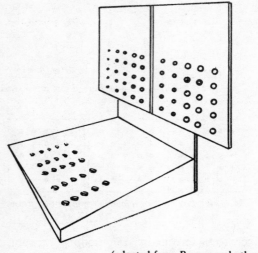

(adapted from Bruner and others, 1966)

Figure 4.6 Olson's apparatus for investigating strategies

determine which of the diagrams represented the configuration on the board. He had to discover this by testing his own switches, but was asked to do so with the minimum number of presses of the switches. Some children were tested under 'free' conditions in which they pressed as many switches as they wished until they had the answer. Others worked under a 'constrained' condition, in which each press was followed by a query 'now do you know which of the switches is the correct one?'. The purpose of this being to emphasise the need to use as few presses as possible, and to examine the differences between how children *would* perform and *could* perform.

Figures 4.7 and 4.8 show two of the patterns used. In the former only two possibilities were offered and only one press was needed to gain the necessary information, in the latter two presses were needed. Examination of the children's responses showed that nearly all of them were constantly using one of three possible strategies. These were:

SEARCH: presses independent of the diagrams; off-pattern switches as likely to be pressed as on-pattern ones; no particular bulb seen as informative and solution often not reached.
SUCCESSIVE PATTERN MATCHING: switches pressed which are part of the pattern for one or both models; on-pattern presses are

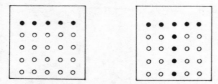

Figure 4.7 Pattern discrimination requiring single press

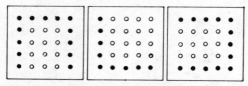

Figure 4.8 Pattern discrimination requiring two presses

no more likely to be informative than redundant; subject begins at pressing for one pattern, whether it permits discrimination or not; an attempt is made to trace a complete pattern, taking a large number of trials; time per trial is short as strategy is externalised into action.

INFORMATION SELECTION: switches on-pattern are pressed more than those off-pattern; on-pattern informative switches pressed earlier and more often than on-pattern redundant switches; time per trial is long as the task is internalised.

Analysis of strategies employed at different ages indicated a very marked developmental trend. Under free conditions all the three-year-olds used the most primitive *search* strategy. Children of five and seven years used the *pattern* strategy almost exclusively, and it was only the nine-year-olds who displayed the *informative* strategy, and then in only about 20 per cent of the responses.

Under constrained conditions the development appeared much more quickly, suggesting that children may have competences which they do not spontaneously employ. With this group some children used a *pattern* strategy at age three years and the *informative* strategy constituted 20 per cent of the responses at five years, 80 per cent at seven years and 100 per cent at nine years.

Olson concluded

One is struck ... by the fact that there is a very large gap between what children conventionally do and what they are capable of doing. Constraining the children to a more careful use of information leads them to far more sophisticated strategies than we would have anticipated from observing their behaviour in the absence of constraint. It is hard to find problems that are impossible for a child, given some coaching and some external aids.

Developmental trends do not result in a final, adult system for concept attainment. In their study with adult subjects Bruner *et al* (1956) demonstrated that there were several characteristic strategies with which individuals would tackle a complex problem. In this case the material comprised an array of cards, each bearing instances of four attributes, one, two or three squares, circles or crosses, coloured either red, green or black and surrounded by one, two or three borders (Figure 4.9). From these it is possible to categorise groups of cards as exemplars of a particular concept; for instance, 'all red cards with borders', 'all cards which are not green' and 'all cards with either three figures or three borders, but not both'. It is clear that concepts can differ both in their level of generality and in the manner in which criteria have been employed to produce them. Bruner distinguished between three categories of concept:

Conjunctive: defined by the *joint presence* of appropriate values of several attributes (e.g. those which are red, carry circles, and have no borders).

Disjunctive: defined by a specific class or any instance of a

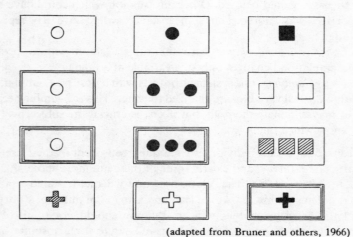

(adapted from Bruner and others, 1966)

Figue 4.9 Sample from Bruner's card array

constituent of that class (e.g. all cards with three red circles, or three red figures, or three figures, or red figures, or three circles, or circles, or which are not red).

Relational: defined by the presence of a specific relationship between attributes (e.g. those having equal numbers of borders and figures).

He pointed out that the use of these different criteria on any given array of stimuli can result in some of the items being included in quite different classes, and that there is nothing intrinsic within the item itself which suggests how it should be classified.

In the experiment subjects were presented with one card from the array and were told that it was an exemplar of a particular concept which the experimenter had in mind. Subjects were then asked to select cards and to enquire whether they were examples or not, so that they could determine which concept was being employed. The analysis revealed four possible strategies:

Simultaneous Scanning: in which each selection is used to deduce which hypotheses are still valid. Because the composite of attributes in the target concept is one of many, the strain of keeping all possible concepts in memory is very considerable, as is the deductive process needed to treat each case.

Successive Scanning: this also requires the testing of one hypothesis at a time. In this case only the information upon which the subjects focussed would be used. Other information which could have been derived was ignored. Thus some instances would have to be repeated later.

Conservative Focussing: here the subject starts with a positive exemplar and changes only one variable at a time.

Focus Gambling: this system also starts with a positive exemplar, but now several variables are changed together. This is a gamble because it may eliminate them all, but if one is crucial the subject will not know which one it was.

Bruner found that individuals were quite consistent in their use of a particular strategy, and clearly some of these are more successful and more arduous than others. We do not know whether repeated exposure to problems of this sort would lead adults to adopt different strategies, but the experiment does indicate that we should not think of the cognitive development of the child as moving to some absolute, adult level of competence. Did different childhood experiences lead to different adult strategies? We do not have the answer to this question either.

The Work of Jean Piaget

Jean Piaget was Professor of Experimental Psychology at the University of Geneva. For most of his adult life he developed and refined his theory of how the intellect develops as the child copes with his environment. His work has had a profound effect upon educational thought in most western countries.

Piaget referred to his work as *genetic epistemology*. Epistemology is the study of the structure of knowledge, and the adjective *genetic* indicates that his interest was in its origins and the ways in which it develops. His early training as a biologist led him to the view that the basic laws which govern the physical activity of living organisms may well be similar to those which govern intellectual activity.

If one considers the amoeba, a microscopic, single-cell animal living in water, one can discern a close relationship between the changes which occur in the organism and objects which exist in its environment. Thus, to trap a particle of food the animal shapes its body into two long processes (pseudopoda) which encircle the particle and draw it into the cell, possibly breaking it up and distributing it inside the cell. Having taken in the food the amoeba now has to utilise it, that is make it a part of itself. To do this it produces digestive enzymes which will dissolve the nutrients. Waste products will then be pushed out through the cell wall. Piaget believed that these two complementary activities, taking-in (assimilation) and changing-in-order-to-make-use-of (accommodation) are fundamental processes in intellectual development too.

An analogous situation arises in the intellectual development of a child. Imagine a young boy, Peter, who has a brother, Mike. To Peter the term 'brother' may refer solely to Mike; that is, 'Mike' and 'brother' are synonymous. If Peter is now informed that John also has a brother, Tim, he may assimilate this information. That is, he may 'take it in', although the act of perception is not a passive one. The information may be substantially modified and restructured as Peter reproduces it in his own mind. Having assimilated the information, Peter may not be able to use it because it confounds his existing notion 'brother' = 'Mike'. In order to use it he must adjust his existing concept of *brother*; that is, he must accommodate to it, just as the amoeba adjusted to utilise the food. Peter then ends up with a new and more sophisticated concept of *brother*.

The individual's encounters with his environment are determined, according to Piaget's theory, by inherited mechanisms which are common to the whole species. They are called *functional invariants*. See Fig 4.10. Piaget believed that all mankind is endowed with an intellect which is organised. Additionally, when an individual manifests intelligent behaviour he is demonstrating an adaptation to environmental phenomena, and this adaptation is made up of the two complementary processes of accommodation and assimilation. Organisation and adaptation are termed functional invariants. Whereas the functions are invariant, at any particular stage in the child's life his actions will be somewhat variable, though they will be seen to have certain unifying features. That is, he will be operating with a series of mental structures which are commensurate with his present level of understanding and experience. These will be formed by the action of organisational and adaptational processes introducing new material into the existing structures, causing them to be reorganised. The system is fundamentally hierarchical. Each reorganisation is dependent upon the existence of the previous stage and it is impossible for stages to be omitted. Thus, in a very crude sense, children of a given age are more likely to demonstrate similarity of structures than children of different ages. It is this aspect of Piagetian theory which is most commonly emphasised, and which is often referred to as the 'ages and stages approach'. However, it should be remembered that this is only the intermediate portion of the overall theory.

This intermediate or structural portion of the theory concerns detail which is obviously more variable than the function aspect, but it is, nonetheless, relatively common at any given time in the life span. The content may be even more variable between children as it represents the raw data which they experience in order to gain knowledge. Clearly this will be heavily influenced by cultural and chance factors, so we would not expect any necessary similarities between the experiences of different people. Yet within a relatively homogeneous culture we might still expect children to have very many shared experiences, though Piaget's theory does not pre-suppose it.

At any particular time the child will be operating with a set of behaviour patterns (or schemes) which belong to a characteristic structure. But Piaget's theory is essentially a dynamic one, and so it is necessary to

Functional Invariants (common to all mental activity)		Structures (common to a stage of development)	Content (possibly unique)
organisation		e.g. concrete operations	e.g. responses to questions involving estimation of quantity, time etc.
adaptation {	accommodation assimilation		

Figure 4.10 Levels of abstraction in Piaget's model

explain why this structure should be superseded by another. To accomplish this he introduces the concept of *equilibration*. When the child is presented with a number of novel features of his environment he will attempt to understand them by internally representing them in his memory (assimilation) and by trying to organise his mental category systems so that the new piece of information fits with others it already has stored (accommodation). As we saw in the example given earlier the child may find this impossible, the new information simply will not fit. He then experiences disequilibrium, and will strive until a new equilibrium is reached and the mental tension is resolved. But in time this too may be found inadequate, and the process will be repeated until yet higher level structures are achieved. Sometimes one state of equilibrium may be very short-lived, in which case a child might move through two stages very rapidly, whilst another may stick on one level for a considerable time; but the order in which the stages are achieved is invariant, and, in general, the characteristics of any given stage can be linked to specific ages of an average child. We shall now consider the details of these stages more closely.

The sensori-motor stage (0 to 2 years)

We have already used the term *action* to mean the way in which the child deals with experiences. In this stage the term can be used literally, as the infant is restricted to motor activities in his manipulation of his environment. That is, he is unable to internalise a representation of an object, but symbolises it in the form of physical action. Close similarities will be seen between this and what Bruner called enactive representation (p. 63). However, even the most cursory observer of infants will be aware that there are enormous differences between the capabilities of the new-born and the two-year-old, and Piaget described many of these, whilst maintaining that the fundamental structure is still sensori-motor in nature.

The infant is certainly not restricted to only believing in the permanence of an object which is held, nor even one that is in sight. After only a few months it will seek and find objects which are placed out of sight under cushions. So already we have a clear example of emancipation from perception – 'I cannot see it yet I know that it is there'.

At first the child seems to be unable to differentiate thinking about an object from acting upon it. That is, he can only solve simple problems by acting out his own responses to those objects. Piaget described how his daughter, on dropping a rattle, waved her arm more and more energetically apparently in an attempt to reproduce the rattling noise. During the second year the child moves toward internal representations which do not require this activity. Such an internalised process is termed a *pre-operation*. Pre-operational thought requires that the child form some symbol which can represent an object in his mind. When such symbolism is becoming established Piaget concluded that the second stage has been reached.

The pre-operational stage (2 to 7 years)

Pre-operational thought is severely limited, yet it is a distinct advance on the previous stage. The child is able to represent the environment in symbolic form and to distinguish between himself and objects in the world around him. Both his language and his thought are characterised by *egocentrism*. In everyday language this term is perjorative, and denotes someone who is selfish and self-centred, but Piaget used it as a simple description. The child is 'self-centred' in the literal sense that he is unable to comprehend the view other people may possess. He acts and speaks on the assumption that what is known to him must be common knowledge to all. This is clearly manifest when a young child attempts to recount an episode which he has experienced. Usually he does not attempt to set the scene or describe the participants, but assumes the listener already knows these.

A classical experiment to illustrate this phenomena is the 'three mountain problem'. The subject is shown models of three mountains, set out in front of him as shown in Figure 4.11.

When a doll is placed in some position other than that from which the child views the scene, the subject is unable to identify which view the

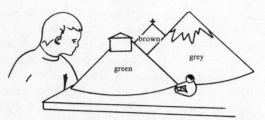

Figure 4.11 Apparatus for the 'three mountain problem'

doll will have, and he cannot rearrange the mountains to reproduce the view which the doll has.

Pre-operational thinking is also limited to handling only one attribute of a stimulus at a time, and it is usually very obvious physical attributes. For instance, if five coins and five sweets are laid out in a row, with a coin against each sweet, the child will readily agree that there are the same number of coins as sweets. If the coins are now spread out, so that the row extends beyond the row of sweets he is likely to declare that there are now more coins than sweets, even though he knows that none was added or subtracted. This is because he is influenced by one obtrusive dimension, the length of the row, and he uses this as an index of 'more than' and 'less than'. He is also unable to master the idea that, if none has been added or subtracted the number is still the same. This idea, known as conservation, will arrive with the next stage, but until it does, the child is still dominated by his perceptions in such tasks.

Failure to conserve is also indicated by a number of experiments, amongst which is one involving estimation of volume. If two identical jars are filled with equal quantities of water, so that the water levels are equal, the pre-operational child will agree that there is the same amount of liquid in each jar. When the contents of one jar are then poured into a shorter wider jar, so that the height of the water is less, he will say that the taller column of water is the greater amount even though the pouring was done in front of him. Again, he is being influenced by a single predominant attribute, the height of the column. He has failed to comprehend conservation of volume, which is bound up with what Piaget referred to as *The Principle of Reversibility*. This principle, when it is mastered, enables the child to mentally undo the process. In this case it would involve mentally recognising that if the water was poured back into the tall jar again, the heights would still be the same.

Some time in the seventh or eighth year most children will experience a state of disequilibrium with problems of this sort. Whereas the child of five will assert that the amounts in the jars are the same, then different, with no sign of perplexity, a little later responses will be hesitant and cautious. Bruner (1964) refers to this as a mismatch between language and thought, and indeed this does seem to be a good description. Usually, if pressed, the child will revert to a pre-operational decision, but it is quite clear that something is happening to his perception of the problem. Piaget believed that the structure is in disequilibrium and is about to be replaced by another stage, that of concrete operations.

Concrete operations (7 to 11 years)

The emergence of operational thinking denotes yet a further emancipation from the here-and-now perceptions of a problem situation. Flavell (1963), perhaps the most cogent commentator on Piagetian Theory, describes the difference between the pre-operational and operational thinker in the following way. 'It is simply that the older child seems to have at his command a coherent and integrated cognitive *system* with which he organises and manipulates the world around him'.

Concrete operational thought is less egocentric, and is able to conserve such qualities as volume, length and weight by application of the principle of reversibility. In addition to this understanding of conservation there develops an ability to classify objects according to some particular characteristics, and to build these classifications into complex networks of subordinate and superordinate categories. Thus *mother* and *father* now refer not only to two specific beings but to two whole classes of adults. These classes can also be added to produce a superordinate class of *parents*, parents can be seen as a larger class than *mothers* so that a whole series of logical transformations is possible. It has been suggested (Piaget, 1950) that the symbols $+, -, \times, +, =, <, >$, etc., symbolise these transformations and represent the types of action which belong to this domain of operations.

The limitations of the child's thinking are due to his dependence upon concrete objects about which he can think. This does not mean that he must actually manipulate objects in order to solve problems concerning them, but he must be able to represent them as images in his mind. He is not yet able to work with the abstractions of algebra, although he can perform calculations with first order abstractions where x and y represent known concrete objects such as *apples* and *pears*. Nor is he able to set up an hypothesis and systematically test it, for this is the distinguishing characteristic of the next stage of intellectual development.

Formal operations (from 11 years)

This, the final stage of intellectual development, was initially thought to commence at about the age of eleven years. Several commentators have suggested that this is a rather early estimate however, and latterly Piaget himself (1972) indicated that this is probably so. Furthermore it seems highly probable that some individuals may never reach this stage, and it seems unlikely that anyone operates consistently at such a high level. However, as an indication of the type of thinking which a normal adolescent might achieve it deserves closer examination. We turn to Flavell (1963) for a general description.

> The most important general property of formal operational thought ... concerns the real versus the possible. Unlike the concrete operational child, the adolescent begins his consideration of the problem at hand by trying to envisage all the possible relationships which could hold true in the data and then attempts, through a combination of experimentation and logical analysis, to find out which of these possible relations in fact do hold true.

Whereas concrete operations were concerned with producing equilibrium based upon what came directly to the senses, formal operations concern themselves with potentialities, with imagining what might exist and how it might be acted upon. This is true hypothetico-deductive reasoning, the ability to set up an hypothesis of what might be the case, and then systematically to determine whether it is so.

Those classifications of concrete stimuli, produced in the previous stage of development, are now used as raw data from which the child makes wider, more general logical connections.

The Pendulum Experiment is one which has been used to examine the transition from concrete to formal operations. The child is presented with a stand, lengths of thread and several different weights. His task is to determine whether it is the length of thread, the weight on the end, or the height from which the weight is released which influences the period of the pendulum (the time taken for one complete oscillation). Younger children act in a sensible way in that they vary attributes of the system in order to discover different consequences, but their behaviour is unsystematic in that they are unable to disembody the general features, such as weight, length, etc., from the impact of the actual objects upon their senses. Therefore they tend to vary two or more attributes at a time, and the sensory data presented by the weights results in children at the concrete operational stage having great difficulty in 'excluding the weight factor ... they generally find 'good' reasons to justify the influence of weight' (Piaget and Inhelder, 1969).

In contrast, some adolescents can dissociate the factors of the problem from the individual attributes of specific objects and are able to vary them systematically until a conclusion is reached.

Piaget's work has enjoyed great popularity for several decades. Indeed in the field of teacher education, particularly at the primary school level, it has assumed the role of pedagogic orthodoxy. There are a number of criticisms which have been made of his work, however, and it is now appropriate to consider these.

Critical Notes on Piaget's Theory

One criticism refers to the methods used in obtaining data. It has been argued that his samples of children were small and unrepresentative, being mostly drawn from upper middle class families in a Western culture. This is certainly a weakness, breaking the usual rules which many psychologists seek to apply to their research, but it is perhaps not a particularly serious criticism now. Large numbers of replication studies have been carried out in many cultures (see Lovell, 1964; Lunzer, 1960; Smedslund, 1961), and whilst some differences are noteworthy the general consensus is that those aspects of child behaviour which Piaget identified do indeed exist in children in general.

A further criticism relates to the specific methods used in the studies. Piaget's technique was essentially 'clinical' in that each child's thought patterns were traced by a series of questions, each being dependent upon the previous response given by the child. This contrasts with the controlled experimental technique which demands absolute uniformity of treatment for all subjects in a sample. This criticism is somewhat cogent. It would be absurd to deny the clinical approach a place in psychological research. At different times people have sought to reject data from introspection, dreams, intuition and many other difficult-to-control processes. Inevitably psychology has been the poorer for their exclusion. These can only offer one type of evidence however; they are rich sources of hypotheses. Subsequently a more rigorous technique is needed to establish that hypotheses derived from such data are plausible and *the most likely* explanations of the phenomena. Further psychological experiments should set out to test the ideas in such a way that all other possible explanations are eliminated. It has been argued that Piaget did not satisfy this latter requirement (Bower, 1974; Bryant, 1974; Donaldson, 1978). Piaget's observations demonstrated that the phenomena he observed were consonant with his over-all theory, but his methods did not systematically exclude alternative explanations. (See Brown and Desforges, 1979, for an extensive critique).

The Work of Bryant and Donaldson

We shall examine one of Bryant's studies in more detail. Piaget showed children a stick A which was longer than another B. He then removed A and showed the child stick B alongside a stick C, which was shorter still. So the child had seen $A>B$ and $B>C$. He observed that young children could not make the inference that $A>C$, whereas the older children (at about seven to eight years) could. He concluded that the inability to make such inferences was due to the mental structures with which younger children operated. Never having seen A alongside C, and being heavily dominated by perceptual cues, they were unable to make the necessary link between A and C.

Bryant pointed out how crucial it was that we be sure of this phenomenon.

> There would be little point, for example, in teaching such a child to use a ruler, because he will have no conception that different things could be compared with each other through their common relations to it.

He saw two possible alternative explanations. First, that the younger children simply forgot about the magnitude of A once it was removed from sight. So he set about ensuring that his subjects did not have a memory failure before they proceeded with the experiment. Secondly, he was concerned to ensure that children who were ostensibly making the correct inference were not simply 'parroting' a formula. It will be recalled that A was only ever seen in a 'longer than' position, and C only in a 'shorter than' position. Therefore it would be possible for a child to repeat 'A is bigger than' and 'C is less than' without really understanding why. To obviate this Bryant extended the sequence to include five

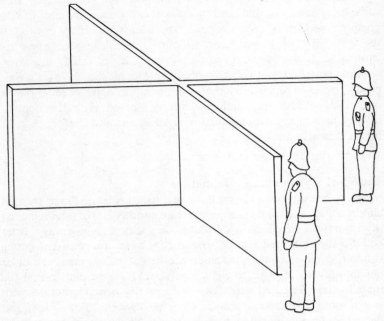

Figure 4.12 Donaldson's apparatus for assessing egocentricity

sticks, $A>B>C>D>E$. Now, when selecting sticks B and D for inference, he was able to use two which had been seen in both 'larger than' and 'shorter than' positions. Under these circumstances he found that children of four years of age achieved very high success rates (82 per cent correct).

We have already seen (p 72–3) that on the basis of the Three Mountain Experiment the Piagetians deduced that young children's thinking was egocentric. Donaldson (1978) explored the possibility that the observed behaviour was a result of the complexity and unfamiliarity of the display, and that a simplified and more familiar set-up would produce different results. Her apparatus is illustrated in Figure 4.12. Two policeman dolls were positioned so that between them they could see into three of the four corners made by the intersecting walls. Young children of 3 and 4 years were then invited to place a child doll so that it could not be seen by either policeman. Children of this age were reported to have no difficulty in doing so. These findings suggest that egocentricity may be an artefact of the experiment, and not a general characteristic of the child's thinking.

Much recent research has been directed towards a re-evaluation of Piaget's theory. There is still a wide divergence of opinion about its validity, and about its implications for educators. There seems to be little dispute that, whatever its shortcomings, it represents one of the most inventive and sophisticated attempts to generate a comprehensive theory of development.

Contemporary educational thought lays great emphasis upon the influence of the early years of development, particularly with regard to the experiences judged most likely to produce sound intellectual performance in middle and late childhood. If is interesting to observe that this is not the inference Flavell (1971) draws from Piaget's work. On the contrary, his view is that in all likelihood genetic factors account for a very high proportion of development in the infant; and that, except in very abnormal circumstances, most young children will satisfactorily pass through the sensori-motor and pre-operational stages without systematic adult intervention. He therefore suggests that educational-ists should concentrate their efforts on the later years of childhood, at which time the differential effects of backgrounds and experiences are likely to prove more crucial.

A Behaviourist View of Concept Formation

Theorists such as Piaget and Vygotsky have adopted what is often called a cognitive view. They employ ideas which are not empirically testable, such as the notion of objects being represented in the mind of the child. Because these cannot be subjected to scientific scrutiny the Behaviourists have avoided these terms, and choose to analyse the behaviour of children in relation to the stimuli presented to them in carefully controlled experimental situations.

In a simple experiment a child might be presented with two stimuli, one display showing a square and the other a circle. If the concept of *circle* is required, he will be rewarded, perhaps with a sweet, every time he selects the circle when the two stimuli are displayed. When the task has been learned, that is when the correct selection is always made, two new stimuli will be shown. The second pair may be a triangle and a circle of different size. If performance on the second pair of stimuli contains fewer wrong selections than the performance of an untrained child it is assumed that the concept has been transferred to some extent.

To eliminate the possibility that transfer occurred simply because the child's ability to discriminate shapes had increased, the experiment can be elaborated. Another group of children could be taught initially with a square and a diamond shape. They should show no improvement when tested with a triangle and a circle if visual discrimination is unchanged.

A more enduring problem is that of ensuring that the child has perceived that the stimulus is a circle, yet a different circle than in the first instance. Transfer could appear to occur if the child thought he was looking at the *same* circle again. To obviate this the transposition experiment was designed. Two stimuli would be selected, one of which more nearly represented a circle. A very thin elongated ellipse and a fatter one might be used. When the child has learned to select the fatter ellipse he is presented with two more stimuli, the fatter ellipse again and one which is more nearly a circle. If he is acquiring a concept of circular the child should now reject the ellipse which was formerly correct and select that which more nearly approximated a circle.

That children could perform transposition tasks led cognitive psychologists to claim responses were not to individual stimuli, but to the relationships between them. These relationships, they maintained, demanded an inner representation of a concept of 'more like a circle'.

Kendler and Kendler (1961) tested children of various ages on tasks of discriminating shape and brightness. Their experiments used a form of transposition known as reversal learning. In this the change from the first pair of stimuli is made by reversing them. That is, if the child has been rewarded for selecting the larger of two figures he is now rewarded for selecting the smaller. Children of between five and six years of age were first trained to select the larger of two rectangles, irrespective of whether it was black or white. They were then randomly divided into two groups. Group 1 had to reverse to selecting the smaller rectangle, Group 2 had to select black (Figure 4.13).

The Kendlers argued that if the concept had been acquired by a straightforward stimulus-response process, Group 2 should learn the new task more quickly, for some of the initial training had quite fortuitously involved rewarding the selection of black rectangles. Group 1 would be at a disadvantage as the selection of smaller rectangles had never been rewarded. On the other hand, if some internal mediation had taken place and the children were representing the idea of 'larger' to themselves, it might be easier for Group 1 to reverse the concept than for Group 2 to generate a new one.

In the sample as a whole neither proved more successful, but when

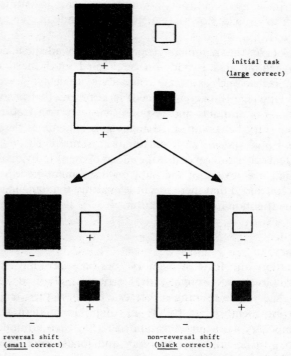

initial task
(<u>large</u> correct)

reversal shift
(<u>small</u> correct)

non-reversal shift
(<u>black</u> correct)

(adapted from Kendler and Kendler, 1962)

Figure 4.13 Reversal and non-reversal shift

the children's speed of learning the initial task was analysed it was discovered that fast learners succeeded in Group 1 and slow learners in Group 2. The authors explained this result by assuming that the fast learners had superior verbal ability and were able to represent a mediating verbal concept to themselves. The slower children had not yet acquired that ability and were obliged to operate on a more primitive and mechanistic stimulus-response process.

There is much that is speculative in such behaviourist formulations. It is not clear whether the discrimination learning procedures adequately reflect the circumstances under which children normally acquire concepts. It is certainly likely that children may enter these experiments with existing concepts, and their task may be one of selecting an appropriate one rather than generating a new concept.

Furthermore many concepts are highly abstract in nature, and it is difficult to visualise how the experimental paradigm could be adapted to teach them.

Blank (1968) has commented upon the lack of adequate definition of language in this area. In addition she pointed out the need to take into account factors such as attention and ability to delay. Nevertheless the use of language (however defined) as a means of transcending the limitations of stimulus and response is a common feature of much contemporary behaviourism. Language is sometimes described as a *second signal system*, a superordinate system of signals which the individual can use to generalise the effects of many individual signals. In an exhaustive review of the data on discrimination learning Wolff (1967) concluded that there was little evidence that language had more than an attention-directing function.

Memory

Fascination with feats of memory goes back certainly as far as the Ancient Greeks and Romans, whose writers emphasised the important role it had in the training of orators. Some of their techniques for improving memory are still to be found in modern texts. Yet in contemporary work on education there has been an understandable tendency to de-emphasise memory and focus upon understanding, which is deemed to be more important. Whilst the reduction in the number of tasks requiring rote memory is probably desirable, there can be little doubt that the good memory is greatly advantageous in most walks of life.

Early scientific studies of memory tended to treat it as a unitary facility. Terms such as "exercising memory" and "strengthening memory" were employed, almost as though memory was analogous to a muscle. Subsequent studies revealed the need for a more precise definition of the underlying processes.

Readers who are familiar with "improve your wordpower" features in magazines will probably be aware that the scores they obtain may not be a very good index of the vocabulary they use when constructing their own writing. For example, to be able to recognise which of the following definitions is correct:

SEQUESTER: (a) to follow   (b) search for
           (c) seclude   (d) interrogate

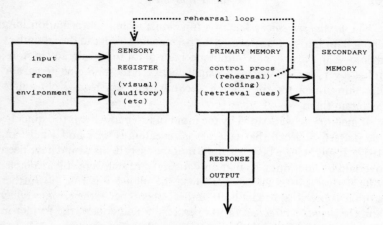

Figure 4.14 Information processing model of memory

does not mean that the word would be recalled at the appropriate point in writing an essay. So to some extent the "strength" of one's memory will depend upon the task set. Usually *recognition* of the appropriate item is an easier process than *recall*. The latter might be described as the recognition of cues which the mind has had to re-create first.

In common with most areas of psychology inference about internal events is derived from observations of external behaviour. So the descriptions of these is an analogy or metaphor, we can never know for sure that this is how things really are. Evidence from a number of sources suggests that at least three general processes are involved in memory (fig. 4.14), although researchers specialising in the study of particular forms of memory, such as that involved in reading, have extensively elaborated the subsystems described here.

The *sensory register* creates an internal representation of the external stimulus. Very little change is made at this point, and the capacity is in excess of what can subsequently be processed in *primary memory*. This rather surprising discovery was made by Sperling (1960) who presented brief exposures of an array of nine letters, having first ascertained that only three could be recalled after such brief times. The letters were in three rows of three, and he then arranged that, as the exposure of the letters terminated, a signal indicated which row should be recalled. In spite of the limitations previously shown, subjects could perform this task and reproduce any row or column of the array. Sperling concluded that the sesory register held the information long enough for a decision about what was to be passed on.

The *primary memory* has two functions; to hold information long enough for it to be transformed for permanent storage in the secondary memory: and to act as an output mechanism for things already in store. It has a very limited capacity, usually between five and nine items, and it retains them for only a few seconds unless *rehearsal* is used to maintain them.

If memory is overloaded by the input of too many items too quickly, the pattern of recall that emerges is revealing (Deese and Kaufman, 1957). It might have been assumed that the early items would have been overlaid by later ones, so that only the most recent were still available. Alternatively, it might be that, once the memory is full, no further storage is possible. In fact both of these phenomena, the *recency effect* and the *primacy effect* seem to operate simultaneously; the former in primary memory and the latter in secondary memory (fig. 4.15). The loss of the middle items is thought to be due to their having been too long in primary store to remain there (and rehearsal prevented by new incoming material), and too little time having been available for the *control processes* to operate, by which items enter the *secondary memory*.

Unlike the primary memory, which operates very much upon the surface features of stimuli, what an item looks like or how it sounds, secondary memory tends to seek economies by linking and clustering items which share some common purpose or meaning. Random lists of words may be re-ordered to produce meaningful groups, or embedded

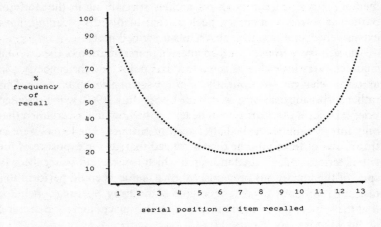

Figure 4.15 serial recall curve

in additional material such as sentence structures in order to link them together logically. *Mnemonics* are strategies which attempt to apply meaning to arbitrary arrays: e.g. Richard of York Gave Battle In Vain, 'I' before 'E' except after 'C' (see Brown *et al*, 1975 for a series of experiments based upon these features of memory).

It will be noted that these mnemonic devices do not actually facilitate immediate recall, but provide lengthier routes via enhanced meaning by which the original stimulus may be *reconstructed*. It is likely that much of our stored memory utilises this form, and that we do not always store records of actual events, but rules and mechanisms by which the events can be recreated. This reconstruction process may often be influenced by other factors, such as our motivational state or our estimate of the probability of such an event occurring. A blurred movement through a steamy window is more likely to be interpreted as a child on a scooter than as a pig on a pogostick.

Developmental Changes In Memory and Metamemory

Sometimes young children astound adults with the amount of detail which they seem to recall of past events. Then, on another occasion, they seem to have forgotten something highly memorable. Whilst it is possible that their memory processes operate only spasmodically, it is not thought that this is so. A more plausible interpretation is that the child does not discriminate between events which he commits to memory in the same way as the adult. There are, however, some differences between the memory of children and adults.

That even very young infants have some memory for past events is indisputable. The discovery that shaking a rattle causes an intriguing noise does not seem to need rediscovery after one or two successful occasions. The anxiety caused by the absence of mother is also a clear indication that her appearance is not only distinctive, but that it can be recalled in her absence; a case of genuine recall rather than recognition. Why adults do not remember very much of their childhood is perplexing. It may be that the manner of storage is less permanent, or that the cues needed for successful recall are no longer available.

Many authorities now believe that the major changes which occur during childhood are not fundamental changes to the memory processes but to the techniques and knowledge which govern their deployment. Understanding one's own memory processes, recognising when tasks require memorisation, and knowing how best to effect memorisation are all part of what is known as *metamemory* (see Kail, 1984).

Earlier it was stated that primary memory had a capacity of around seven items. Children of five or six years often have somewhat less than this, probably around three or four items. By the age of ten years this capacity has risen very close to that of an adult, but whereas teenagers have a fairly good idea of their span, young children often overestimate wildly. Similarly, children of all ages recognise that large amounts of material are harder to remember than small amounts, but younger ones do not relate that to overall capacity. That is, they will judge 2 items to be more difficult than 1, 12 than 6, and 100 than 50, even though the volume is only crucial in the middle instance where it bridges the normal memory span. (Recently a child with learning difficulties responded to the author's question 'If I read out some numbers, how many do you think you could remember in order?' with 'About half of them.' Whether that reflects the same phenomenon, or simply a reasonable guess of how many numbers I would fire at her, is open to conjecture.)

A very important aspect of metamemory is the monitoring of processing to assess its success. There is evidence that this begins before the child starts school, but that it takes some years to become reasonably thorough. Wellman (1977) showed pictures of unfamiliar and familiar objects to children of between six and nine years. They were asked to predict how well they would be able to recognise the names and select the appropriate pictures. Successful monitoring would lead to prediction and recognition agreeing, but if the child predicted success and failed, or predicted failure and succeeded, then monitoring was presumably poor. The author demonstrated that prediction improved considerably as age increased.

The suggestion that memory development is really due to increases in metamemory skills rather than the growth of some basic neurological structures is not without its opponents. If it is true, however, and given that these metamemory skills can be learned, the implications for significant improvements over relatively short periods of time are considerable. However, as Brown (1983) has pointed out, the field of metacognition is still developing, and there is still confusion over what may properly be termed 'metacognition'.

5

Language Development

Describing the speech patterns of an individual, even an articulate adult, is not an easy matter. Simply reporting an utterance often gives very little information unless we are able to convey the emphasis which was placed on particular words (their expressive quality), and the particular context in which they were uttered. There may be a dozen different possible meanings (semantic content) for any single sentence. Consider the following sentence: 'John has a new wife'. If you and I knew John quite well, and I said that to you, what would you understand me to mean? That John had remarried? But John may be still married to the same woman who, on this occasion, has exchanged her customary tweed suit and flat shoes for a slinky gown and modish evening shoes, and whose brown hair had suddenly become very blond. Now the intention is to convey something different. Or perhaps John is paying rather too much attention to another woman in the room. Now the same statement has yet another meaning. There may be much of interest in the way in which the sentence is constructed, and many linguists are concerned with these aspects of language, but there is a great deal more in the semantics of language which is much more difficult to determine. Yet without its meaning a word is just a series of noises.

Having intimated one of the problems which the student of language will encounter, we must now confuse the issue even further by turning our attention to the speech patterns of the child. These will not be in the same form as adult speech and it may often be even more difficult to extricate meaning. That a child does not tell us something in language we understand is not to say that the child himself does not understand that which he wishes to convey. This problem is receiving a great deal of attention from contemporary psychologists (see Blank, 1975; Francis, 1975).

First Sounds

Almost all babies cry. Wolff (1969) observed eighteen babies intensively for one month each in naturalistic surroundings. By analysis of tape recordings and sound spectograms he distinguished hunger cries from anger cries, with a possible further category of gastric pain cries. Apart from being an expression of a physical state the cry has a crucial role as the initiator of some of the earliest social interaction. It will often cause attention to be paid by an adult and cessation of crying may be interpreted by that adult as indicative of a positive reaction to that attention. Adults will also spend a great deal of time talking to an infant even though they realise that he will not understand; but he will certainly respond. Contemporary theorists suggest that the infant may be predisposed to respond to movement and sound which are typical of a human being in their sequences and ranges (Trevarthen, 1975).

Ricks (1972) recorded cries from infants in different situations, when hungry, uncomfortable, etc. He found that parents were able to identify the types of cries of all the babies, including a foreign one; though they were not able to say which were the cries of their own child nor which were those of the foreign child. This suggests that there may be a universal sound-system which serves to communicate basic meanings.

Subsequently the child's utterances are extended to include babbling. This is sometimes referred to as 'baby talk', as though it was a childish attempt to imitate adult speech. This seems rather dubious as it occurs in deaf infants too. Differences occur later, for after a while deaf children will cease to babble whereas the hearing children will gradually introduce more word-like noises. At four to six months *ma, mee* and *na* are common, and these nasal sounds are followed by the plosive *da-da, ba-ba* and *ta-ta*. Ricks (op.cit.) suggests that these 'dada words' are followed by a second type which he calls 'label words'. The latter do not occur in babbling but only in the context of the particular object or action to which they refer. The label words appear to have great importance to the child as they generate a good deal of excitement. Ricks makes the interesting observation that these early words are often adopted by the parents in order to facilitate interaction, an unexpected reversal of influence.

Label words are single utterances, but it is by no means clear that they refer solely to single objects or actions in the child's experience. If they do not, they represent a significant advance in the use of speech.

Holophrastic Speech

We have seen that the first speech of the infant is in the form of single words. Most observers believe that these single words, called holophrases, come to express complex ideas which would most frequently be expressed in a sentence by an adult. This belief is based upon studying the utterances in context and observing the behaviours and expectations which the infant seems to associate with them. Thus the word 'Mama' may be associated with reaching forward and raising the arms in the expectation of being picked up, in which case it might signify 'Mama, please pick me up'. At another time it might be said anxiously, accompanied by consternation or distress, and might mean 'Where has my Mama gone?'

Whilst it seems reasonable to suppose that the holophrase represents complex ideas it would be presumptuous to suggest that they are ideas which are as complete and clear as those in the preceding paragraph. It is very unlikely that young children would have such detailed and differentiated ideas, but it is highly likely that the single word utterance is intended to convey something rather more complex than simply a declaration or a verbal label for an object. McNeill (1970) observes 'A degree of semantic imprecision in holophrastic speech is therefore taken for granted. There remains, however, a question of what it is that children are imprecise about ...' It has already been stated that deductions about the semantics of holophrases are often made because they are accompanied by actions or emotional reactions. And whilst it is generally believed that they do not only refer to objects they obviously do that too. So holophrastic speech has a large measure of the capacity of more advanced forms of speech. It can be used to stimulate action either of the child himself or of another person (conative function), it can accompany and convey an emotional state (expressive function), and it can draw attention to an object by naming it (referential function).

In Chapter 4 (p. 54) it was reported that Lewis (1951) drew inferences concerning the conceptual development of the child from the way in which words were being used to refer to various animals. In similar vein Greenfield (cited by McNeill, op. cit.) has suggested that analysis of her own child's holophrases indicated a progressive emergence of different relations. She inferred from this that different grammatical relationships were being employed by the child. At ten months the child was using holophrases for conative, expressive and referential purposes. At twelve to thirteen months she was asserting the properties of objects, such as 'ha' for a hot cup or an object which might get hot. By the age of fourteen months she was able to indicate the location in which objects might be found, or in which they were customarily placed, e.g. 'nana' to refer to the top of the refrigerator on which bananas had previously been stored. From fifteen to seventeen months the child used holophrases as though they were words embedded in a phrase or sentence; first as the object of a verb ('door' meaning 'close the door'), then as the object of a proposition ('eye' meaning 'water is in my eye') and finally as a subject of a sentence ('baby' meaning 'baby fell down'). Of all the words used the great majority were nouns, and all the rest adjectives. The following phase of language development involves the combination of words into rudimentary phrases. If Greenfield's thesis is correct, the child already has a rudimentary knowledge of grammatical relations with which to commence this process, though it would be possible to argue that the observed sequence was evidence of a systematic exploration and interaction with the environment (in Piagetian terms) instead. Interpretation as a form of grammar is chosen by McNeill as it relates to Chomsky's theories of language acquisition, to which we shall turn later.

Combining Words

Braine (1963) analysed the two-word utterances of young children by a method known as distributional analysis. The purpose of this technique was to determine whether the juxtaposition of words was random or according to some rules. The analysis revealed that words were used in one of two possible ways, either as general words similar to the earlier holophrases, these he termed *open class*, or as members of a smaller pivot class which were used much more often in combination with a variety of open class words. A common pivotal word 'more' could be used before a number of open class words, giving things like 'more swing', 'more sweeties', 'more hot' etc. Other pivotal words may follow open class words, but pivot class words are never used together.

pivot (P)	*open* (O)
more	baby
big	Mummy
see	sweeties
pretty	hot
	ball

| O – P combinations | 'more sweeties, 'seebaby' |
| P – O combinations | 'Mummy pretty', 'hot more' |

Examination of studies in a number of different languages (Slobin, 1971) suggested that something like the pivot-open construction occurred in Bulgarian, French, German, Japanese, Luo (Kenya), Russian, Samoan and Serbian, so it does not seem that the pattern Braine found was dependent upon some peculiarity of the English language. Another possible explanation might be that the child is simply using a condensed form of adult speech. There are two reasons for discounting this. Firstly, Braine recorded over 2,500 different combinations by one child in a month. This would be a phenomenal feat of memory if each one had been heard from an adult and subsequently repeated. Secondly, the pivot-open sequence is frequently a reversal of the adult form; for example, 'allgone dinner' as a regular construction with 'allgone' in a preceding position. In the adult form this would almost always be reversed, as in 'dinner has all gone'. This is not to say that children do not imitate adult utterances, most parents have a fund of anecdotes to the contrary; but it strongly suggests that the division into the two classes of words is a basic restriction in usage imposed by the child. Such restrictions are another example of a child's use of systematic rules for the regularisation of speech, in other words, his use of a grammar.

Pivot-open combination utterances account for quite a high proportion of the utterances of many children; and we have already observed that pivot-pivot combinations seldom occur. Open class words are sometimes used together, however, and these combinations may be inadequate attempts to elaborate ideas with which the pivot-open combination cannot cope. 'Baby-ball' could be an attempt to elaborate one of several semantic relationships, such as 'baby has the ball' (possession), 'this is a baby (small) ball' (attribution), 'there is a baby and there is a ball' (conjunction), etc. Before semantic content is interpretable the child will have to enter the next phase of language development, in which longer utterances are made.

Simple Sentence Construction

Even three-word utterances clearly demonstrate the next developments in language. Children will often make two attempts at a sentence, the first concerned with one aspect of the content, the second with an embellishment of it. So he may say 'want it' ... 'Peter want it' or 'fall down' ... 'baby fall down'. Slobin describes this in the following way: 'It is as if he first prepared one constituent of a longer sentence, and then "plugged it in" to a more complex sentence.' Brown and Bellugi (1964) found similar evidence from analysis of the pauses children made when uttering sentences. Pauses were introduced at specific points which corresponded with the grammatical divisions between constituents of the sentences. They did not occur at points which would have split up particular components. The sentence 'Make the big dog run' would only be broken up around the noun phrase as 'Make ... the big dog ... run', and never as 'Make the big ... dog run'.

The characteristic oddities of children's speech give it appeal to many adults. Typical examples are 'goed', 'comed', 'sheeps', 'foots' etc. By analogy with the way in which older children and adults learn second languages it is tempting to conclude that the child first of all learns a specific rule, and that only later is he able to learn the exceptions to that rule. The rule *add 'ed'* is a good, all-purpose rule which works on the regular verbs of the English language. As it works for 'walk(ed)', 'talk(ed)', 'rais(ed)' etc., why should it not operate for 'go' and 'come'? Similarly plurals can often be made by the addition of 's'. Slobin (op.cit.) avers that this elegant conclusion is, in fact, incorrect. Initially children learn and use the correct form of many of these words, as they are commonly heard in the speech of adults. He believes that they may be learned as separate vocabulary items, independent of other forms of the same words. Later the child becomes aware of a rule for changing tense or forming plurals, and extends this to all words, thus eliminating the correct forms. This unexpected tendency suggests that the human child is particularly sensitive to linguistic patterns, to such an extent that he will cease to use successful language forms that he has heard in adult usage, and which, presumably, have been frequently reinforced by adult approval and successful communication.

Telegraphic Speech

We have seen that the child learns to expand sentences by 'plugging in' additional units. The sentence he first constructs in this manner will be much more informative than his earlier holophrastic speech, but it will still be rather dissimilar to adult forms. Observers have suggested that it is more like the highly condensed language which adults use in telegrams. For this reason it is often referred to as *telegraphic speech*.

Telegrams are an expensive form of communication, so it is necessary to convey as much information in as few words as possible. In a telephone conversation we might inform a relative that 'We crashed the car in Paris. Luckily no-one was hurt but we shall be delayed for a few days.' The same message by telegram might be 'Crashed car Paris; no-one hurt; four days delay.' This reduces the message by ten words, conveys the same content, and saves us money. It will be noted that the words which we have retained are mostly nouns and verbs, and the child's early sentences are usually made up of these too.

Brown and Fraser (1963) analysed the telegraphic speech which children of two and three years of age used when attempting to imitate some simple English sentences. They reported that nouns and verbs were most frequently kept, with some adjectives and pronouns. Articles, prepositions, the copular verb *be* and auxiliary verbs were usually omitted, as were inflections ('shows' for 'showed', 'cup' for 'cups' etc.) They noted that in this latter respect telegraphic speech differs from the telegram form, for adults do not miss inflections.

Brown and Fraser used the linguist's term *contentive* to refer to those words which the child retained. Contentive words are those which frequently make direct reference to objects, people or actions. Those words which were most frequently omitted were termed *functors*, they indicate subtle changes of meaning or mark the grammatical structure of the sentence. In a subsequent report of this, and later work by Brown and Bellugi in 1964, Brown (1973) reports that there is strong evidence that functors are the parts of speech which are most often left out, though some much more than others. Articles and copular verbs may only be correctly imitated in 30 to 40 per cent of the attempts, but pronouns in as many as 70 per cent of the attempts. These exceptions in conjunction with apparently contradictory evidence from analyses of other languages, led him to redefine functors in a number of categories, some of which may exist in telegraphic speech and others which will not. The probability of their presence would be determined by the frequency of usage in adult speech, their *perceptual salience* (i.e. how distinctive they sound, how much stress they are commonly given), and how many different forms they may exist in (e.g. 'I', 'me', 'my', 'mine'). As these three factors would be differently weighted in different languages this would produce dissonant data under the original definition of 'telegraphic' as the absence of certain grammatical clauses, but not if the absence or presence of words in those classes is mediated by the three factors.

Stages in the acquisition of speech are, of course, notional. Just as there is no distinct boundary between the use of holophrases and pivot-open utterances, so there is no sudden cessation of telegraphic utterances. There will be a gradual transition as the telegraphic speech is elaborated by more functors and increasingly complex structure until, by the age of six or seven years, most utterances will be in the adult form. Adults assist in this process in a number of ways. *Expansion* denotes the filling out of telegraphic sentences. When the child says 'Daddy gone work', the mother will probably respond with 'Yes, Daddy has gone to work' thereby presenting a better model for the child to study.

Dale (1972) discusses such influences of maternal speech upon the child's language development. He observes that most adults are conscious of modifying their speech forms when talking to infants, and he identifies a number of other characteristics of this modification, mostly from the work of Brown and Bellugi (1964) and Brown, Cazden and Bellugi (1969).

Prompting or *constituent prompting* consists of transforming questions into forms which may be closer to their deep structure (see p. 104). 'What do you want?', if unanswered, may be changed to 'You want what?' which requires only a single utterance to answer it. Dale opines that many children may initially learn questions in this form.

Echoing occurs when an adult repeats the intelligible portions of the child's speech but replaces unintelligible words with question words 'where', 'who' or 'what'. For example, the child's statement 'I'm going shone' is echoed as 'You're going where?'. This, and the previous processes encourage the child to repeat the utterances in modified form.

Cazden (1965) grouped twelve negro children between the ages of twenty-eight and thirty-eight months who were in nursery school and were from deprived homes. She allocated them to four groups of three. In each group one child received forty minutes deliberate expansion of everything he said, another received well formed sentences related to his own utterances but not expansions of them, and a third received no special treatment. These treatments were referred to as *expansion, expiation* and *control*. A number of measures of language development were used and, somewhat surprisingly, *expiation* produced the greatest gains, with *expansion* only slightly superior in development to those in the *control* group.

Various explanations have been offered for these results (Dale, 1972). It is possible that the *expansions* were incorrect and misrepresented what the children intended. Alternatively, the white dialect of the trainers may have been too unfamiliar to the children. Cazden argued that the reason may have been that richness of verbal stimulation is more important than grammatical structure, and that in expiation it was richer and more varied. Dale's own suggestion was that 100 per cent expansion is not only unrealistic but probably incredibly boring or frustrating, and this may have led to a drop in attention. Some, or all, of these explanations may be correct. The experiment does serve to show how artificially increasing a natural phenomenon may lead to abnormal results instead of an increase in expected effects.

In a recent study of children's understanding of metalanguage Robinson and Robinson (1982) explored the extent to which children recognised that instructions they had received were ambiguous, and to what extent they could construct similar instructions to give to another person. Young children were often sure that they had understood ambiguous statements, and tended to translate "difficult" instructions in terms of the quantity of information presented rather than the extent to which they contained ambiguity. Citing one of their own earlier studies, the authors concluded that the role of parents may be crucial in stimulating self-monitoring by the child in order to disambiguate utterances. Telling the child that his meaning is not clear may be an important initiator of this metacognitive skill.

Reception and Production of Language

All the research discussed above has been concerned with the child's abilities to produce speech. Huttenlocher (1974) points out that there is no reason to suppose that the ability to receive and comprehend speech is necessarily coincident with this process. For language to function at all it is necessary that words must be discriminated and matched against a pattern which the individual has previously stored. Huttenlocher uses a Piagetian term *sound-scheme* to refer to this stored information. For establishing the meaning or a word, however, the sounds must be somehow linked with an internal representation of the object or idea to which they refer, and *object-scheme* or *idea-scheme*. Now the processes involved in speech production work from object-scheme to sound-scheme. When a child says 'doggie' it presumably does so because it has a mental representation of *doggie* which it wishes to convey to another person. So the sound-scheme is selected to match an object-scheme which already exists in the child's mind. When someone says 'doggie' to the child the process is reversed. Now the sound-scheme is registered in the mind and an appropriate object-scheme must be matched to it. Huttenlocher's point is that one of these processes may be rather easier than the other. We may be assuming that a child cannot comprehend an utterance because he does not make similar utterances himself, and this might be totally unwarranted.

In a detailed study of speech reception and production by three children between the ages of ten months and nineteen months, the author claims to have found the suspected asymmetry. She found (1) that the children responded to many more words than they produced, (2) the few words that were produced were not a random selection of the words to which they responded systematically. Furthermore, evidence was presented which suggested that the differences between production and reception could not be wholly explained by a simple inability to articulate known words, for the children produced many word sounds and were able to produce recognisable words.

With reference to the expansion of meanings cited by Lewis (Chapter 4, p. 54) Huttenlocher reported that the activities of her subjects led her to conclude that these occurred *only* in production (which Lewis observed) and not in reception (which he did not test).

Language Development in Later Childhood

So far we have been considering the elaboration of utterances in the first five years of life. Most researchers have done the same, on the supposition that by the age of five years the child has mastered the syntax of his language. However, Carol Chomsky (1969) argues that for the next five years there is an orderly progression in language development which, if not as marked as that in the previous five years, is not insignificant. She argues that because five-year-olds use grammatical utterances which correspond to those of the adult there has been a tendency not to investigate further. By means of games and question-and-answer techniques she was able to determine that in four language constructions tested children made a substantial number of language reception errors.

> *Promise:* having ascertained that the child understands the meaning of the word 'promise' and can act out simple actions like 'Bozo tells Donald to hop up and down', the child is asked to act out 'Bozo promises Donald to hop up and down'. Frequently Donald was moved, suggesting that the child interprets the sentence as though the verb was 'orders' or 'tells'.

Easy to See: having established that the child can say whether a doll is 'hard to see' or 'easy to see', and having demonstrated that they can make it either 'easier' or 'harder to see', a blindfold doll is presented and the same question asked. Many children responded to the question in terms of the doll's blindfold.

Ask/Tell: preliminary testing ensured that the children knew the difference between 'to ask' and 'to tell'. They were then told to 'ask for' or 'tell' information to various dolls. Errors consisted of interpreting all instructions as 'tell' when the information was known to child.

Pronouns: the children were given a number of sentences about two dolls and asked to whom the pronouns referred, e.g. 'He knew that Pluto was sad' and 'Micky said he was hungry'. Failure was the incorrect assigning of reference.

Carol Chomsky found that the sequence of achievements on the tests was usually the same, though the age at which success occurred was very variable. Success at *pronouns* occurred at about five years six months, at *promise* and *easy to see* it was mixed from five years six months until nine years, and at *ask/tell* it was mixed at all ages.

The author concludes that there are two aspects to the knowledge of a word in one's language. The first concerns the concept attached to the word, and this her children already had; the second concerns the grammatical constructions into which it can enter, and this the children did not have. Carol Chomsky is certainly correct in maintaining that grammatical developments occur in the second five years of life, although it is probably fair to say that the deficiencies she demonstrated are in the understanding of exceptional grammatical structures. It is still remarkable that most of the general rules which make speech coherent and intelligible are possessed by most five-year-olds.

Theories of Language Acquisition

No other species of animal has a language. Many are able to communicate by the emission of signals, which others in the same species can interpret in the sense that they can modify their behaviour in accordance with these signals. Honey bees, for instance, are thought to perform movements which stimulate others to travel specific distances in given directions to the location of food sources. It seems likely that these events do not depend upon any specific intent on the part of the bees, and furthermore the signals are of limited utility and cannot be compounded or transformed in any creative way to convey additional or novel information. Human language, on the other hand, does have these characteristics. With between fifteen and eighty-five elementary sounds, called *phonemes*, each human language can create many thousands of *morphemes*, forms such as words, parts of words, or letters affixed to words. Morphemes are meaningful entities, whereas the phonemes which comprise them are not. With these morphemes vast amounts of information can be transmitted. Man's exclusive possession of language has puzzled researchers for a long time. Many animals are superior in physical strength and agility, have similar capacity for expressive gesture, and similar brain to body ratios, yet they seem incapable of developing more than a few dozen signals. The apes are our closest relatives in the animal kingdom, and several researchers have attempted to rear chimpanzees as human children in order to ascertain whether environmental or biological factors are responsible for this deficiency. In 1965 R. Brown reported that, in spite of being given far larger amounts of explicit language training than children ever receive the chimpanzees have not learned to speak the family language. Over the past two decades since Brown made that statement there have been several intensive, long-term attempts to obtain improved performances. True, no chimp can 'speak the family language', but Gardner and Gardner reported that their chimp, Washoe, learned a sign language which enabled her to generate meaningful original utterances (Gardner and Gardner, 1971), and since then there have been several cases where the construction of limited word strings has been interpretable as indicative of the use of novel language structures to express events. In a detailed analysis of Washoe's utterances McNeill (1973) suggests that although her language acquisition pattern has much in common with that of humans it may be an incorrect assumption to see her as a representative of a species which is following the same developmental path somewhat slowly. Some fundamental differences in grammar lead him to postulate that

> If man's capacity for language itself is in part a biological adaptation to a certain range of life conditions, it is possible that another species has developed an adaptation to accomplish similar communicative effects under different life conditions.

Whether language is exclusively human or not it is beginning to look as though there is a very strong biological component determining the manner in which it evolves. Views as to the potency of this genetic influence differ, though there is no doubt that, whatever the propensity, no language is acquired without interaction with the environment. Even the special understanding and shared meanings between twins can cause them to be somewhat slow in acquiring normal language (Luria and Yudovitch, 1959). Various theories have been proposed to explain how this interaction with the environment gives rise to language.

Behaviourist Theory

Behaviourists have attempted to explain the language acquisition process in terms of classical and operant conditioning. In the former an utterance becomes paired with a stimulus and response which the child already possesses. According to this theory the child, on being presented with the feeding bottle, may continually hear the parent say 'drink'. It will gradually become conditioned so that part of the total response to the bottle (sucking, holding, quenching thirst) is aroused when the word 'drink' is heard, even in the absence of the actual bottle. These portions of the total response are assumed to be internal and to represent the *meaning* of the word.

Operant conditioning has been more commonly used to attempt to explain the manner in which words come to be uttered in specific contexts. The explanation hinges upon the fact that acts which are reinforced or rewarded in some way are likely to be repeated. Figure 5.1 indicates how this might occur.

Skinner (1957) proposed a much more detailed and elaborate explanation based upon the same fundamental process. He proposed that the reinforced behaviours (or operants) took one of three forms. An utterance which asked for something would be reinforced if whatever was asked for was produced. This type of utterance he termed a *mand*. Utterances such as that shown in figure 5.1. are naming behaviours which are rewarded by parental approval and pleasure. These Skinner termed *tacts*. A further class of operants were those which for the child reinforced by self-stimulation. Repetition of invented sounds or sounds uttered by adults would be the source of these *echoic responses*. By repeating them to his own satisfaction the child would be reinforcing himself. These processes of operant conditioning often achieved success by shaping behaviour toward some desired outcome. When training animals it is not necessary to reward only those behaviours which are perfectly correct. In the early stages rewards may be given for fairly crude approximations to the desired act.

(a) infant learns to utter sounds at will.

(b) infant has tendency to imitate mother or is reinforced for accidental imitation.

(c) imitation occurs in presence of referent.

(d) utterance elicited by referent alone.

Figure 5.1 A behaviourist model of language acquisition

Parents appear to operate a rather similar system, though perhaps not often consciously. Whereas father may register delight at 'de' from his six month old child, he may require something more like 'dada' before his one-year-old delights him.

Markov Processes

In attempting to explain the construction of sentences, Markov processes have been widely used. They appeal to behaviourists because they employ a simple law of association. The process is also referred to as a left-to-right probabilistic model, and implies that the occurrence of each word in the sentence is determined by those words which immediately precede it. The sentence 'He hit the big boy' is then explained by suggesting that the syntax, based upon probability, requires a verb after 'he' and when this verb is active one is led to expect an object towards which it is directed.

If human language consisted exclusively of such relatively simple sentence structures, this explanation would be an elegant way of describing the rules the child learned for the construction of his own utterances. Unfortunately this is not the case. Chomsky (1957) has elaborated upon the deficiencies of the system at length. It will suffice to repeat one or two of his comments here.

By examination of existing language it is possible to determine which words might be expected to follow others. One can then generate a 'sentence' with a very high left-to-right association probability. There is no guarantee that it will be a sentence however. 'Looks at once upon the sky blue bells ring' obeys the rules. An even stronger criticism is that many sentences are constructions in which simple sentences are embedded in others, often separating words which depend upon distant words for their forms. Thus, in the sentence 'The soldier who had told the man to shoot went away', 'Went away' is dependent upon 'the soldier' yet they are separated by a whole embedded sentence.

Many sentences may appear very similar in isolation, yet the listener usually knows what is intended. 'They are reading books' may mean [They] [are reading] [books] or [They] [are] [reading books]. In the previous paragraph we discussed embedded sentences, now we see that sentences also have different phrase constructions. This notion of hierarchies of embedded pieces of language gave rise to another theory of grammar, the Phrase Structure Theory.

The behaviourist explanation has been very strongly criticised, particularly by Chomsky (1959). It is argued that it does not explain how children are able to produce large numbers of novel utterances. With a basic vocabulary of a few thousand words the child is able to create many correct sentences which he has not heard before. This is related to another criticism; that it is impossible to define the semantic content of a sentence in terms of its constituent words.

We have already seen that the meaning was thought to be acquired by conditioning the word to some stimulus-response bond which already existed. However, this would seem to restrict the meaning greatly, and words can mean different things in different contexts. How could it explain the differences we readily perceive in (a) the seal balanced a ball on its nose, (b) the seal was fixed to the letter. Many theorists support the view that the construction of sentences is dependent upon something more sophisticated than the stringing together of words.

In tracing the development of utterances in the first few years it was clear that children's language differed from adult forms in some very significant ways. Furthermore progress did not always mean a close approximation to the adult form. This is further reason to suspect the behaviour-shaping explanation. Syntactic theories are radically different and we shall examine them in more detail.

Phrase Structure Grammar

It was noted earlier that Brown and Bellugi (1964) discovered that children sometimes hesitated between phrases of an utterance, but not within phrases. This led them to suggest that sentence construction was a process of 'plugging in' smaller units. Phrase Structure Grammar is really an elaboration of this idea. Some portions of a sentence seem, intuitively, to have coherence and meaning when taken out of the sentence. 'The lady boiled the cabbage' seems to have units such as [The lady] and [the cabbage], but [lady boiled] is not such a unit. Miller (1962) suggested that the units can be identified as those portions which can be replaced by a single word, as:

The lady	boiled	the cabbage
She	boiled	it
She	cooked	

This process is known as constituent analysis. Each of the units in the sentence is a constituent, but 'lady boiled' is not. Usually the analysis is done in terms of the type of constituent, so that the result is in general terms of the relationships rather than those particular to the one sentence under analysis.

The	lady	boiled	the	cabbage
T	N		T	N
NP		V	NP	
		VP		

The theory suggests that there are rules which would enable the child to construct basic units such as *noun phrases* (NP) out of an *article* (T) and a *noun* (N); and slightly more complex *verb phrases* out of *verbs* (V) and *noun phrases*; and sentences out of composites of *noun phrases* and *verb phrases*. It is these rules which would constitute a phrase structure grammar.

The advangage of this model is that it can cope with the problem of embedded sentences. At any time we can insert an embedded sentence, and the rules which operate allow the sentence to be modified to accommodate it. Only a relatively small number of rules would be needed, yet they could generate an infinite number of products.

Whilst phrase structure grammar offers some plausible ideas about the construction of sentences, it is only dealing with the more observable aspects of language. At another level there is the problem of relating the utterances to the actual ideas which they attempt to convey. 'The lady boiled the cabbage' and 'What did the lady boil?' have totally different phrase structures. Yet they have a good deal of semantic content in common. In order to bridge this gap Chomsky suggests that we must add another set of rules to those of phrase structure grammar, the rules of a transformational grammar.

Generative Linguistics

Chomsky (1957) has been extremely influential in the development of an alternative view of the nature of language and the means by which it is acquired. His ideas are complex and it is possible to give only a very general description here. More detailed treatments are available in Greene (1972), Lyons (1970) and Slobin (1971).

The theory is based upon a rationalist view of language. That is, one which argues the logical necessity of a model of language which can account for the fact that all humans, except a few with specific brain damage, have language, whereas no animals do; that children derive a structured native language from limited exposure to adult speech, some of which may be incomprehensible or incomplete; that children can generate new sentences of their own; and that different languages appear to possess very similar underlying structures. Chomsky's theory suggests the existence in men of a universal *competence* for the acquisition of language. Competence enables the child to sift out from the speech of others the general rules or *grammar* which determine how sentences are constructed. The theory is distinct from an empirical one, which would derive its models from analyses of actual speech utterances. Chomsky refers to these utterances as *performance*. They are produced from the individual's grammar, but are less than perfect because of other factors, such as memory capacity, attention span, vocal apparatus etc.

All natural languages are produced by the rules of the basic grammar, which native speakers will not be conscious of possessing. The grammar can *generate* an immeasurably large number of correct sentences, which constitute a language, and these would be instantly recognised as correct. However, only a small proportion will actually be uttered. Sentences are constructed which are judged to be either correct or grammatically or semantically incorrect, and the criterion for this judgement is the native speaker's intuition. By examining sentences which are judged incorrect, or by constructing sentences which appear similar but have very different meanings, Chomsky attempts to define this linguistic intuition. For example, why do we accept 'the dog looks terrifying', but not 'the dog looks barking', and how do we know that the two apparently similar sentences 'John is easy to please' and 'John is eager to please' convey that 'John' is the object of one and the subject of the other?

We could say that the last two sentences appear similar only on the surface, and this is a term which Chomsky uses. He distinguishes between the *surface structures*, which in this case are similar, and the *deep structures* from which they were derived. The deep structure of 'John is easy to please' would denote the position of 'John' as object, perhaps in some form like 'people can easily please John'. In the second sentence the deep structure might be of the form 'John is eager to please people'. In this case the deep structures have been written as full sentences in order to convey the meaning, but it is not necessarily so. Deep structures may consist of juxtapositions of symbols which only become recognisable sentences when certain *rules* are applied to them. Deep structure, then, conveys the semantic component of an utterance, surface structure conveys its grammatical construction (Figure 5.2).

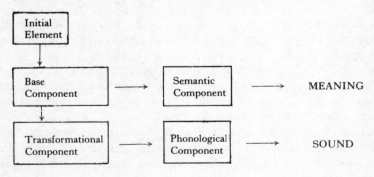

Figure 5.2 Relationships in Chomsky's model of language

The rules to which reference has just been made are the central theme of Chomsky's theory. Linguistic competence is seen as a finite set of rules comprising a *syntax* which enables the meanings of the deep structure to be represented in the phonetic surface structure of the sentence. It is acquired by means of a Language Acquisition Device (LAD) (Chomsky, 1965) which is presumed to be an innate mechanism which is 'tuned' to extract the syntax from the many imperfect and incomplete utterances which the child hears. As performance is wholly dependent upon competence there is no possibility, in terms of this theory, that language could be acquired by any conditioning process acting upon the utterances produced by the child. It is sometimes suggested that competence must consist of specific universal features of language such as the relationships between subject and predicate, or verb and object. Yet this is perhaps emphasising too strongly the language aspect of deep structure. It seems more likely that the juxtaposition of symbols at this level may be simply a facet of the general conceptual development of the individual. In this case a fragment of deep structure such as 'hit the ball' does not so much denote a knowledge of *verb-object* as a knowledge that *acts* can be direct towards *objects*. We are then looking at the child's conception of activity rather than at a specific innate linguistic idea.

'Thus it may well be that the general features of language structure reflect ... the general characteristics of one's capacity to acquire knowledge ...' (1965). Stated in this way the theory appears to have some affinity with that proposed by Piaget (Chapter 4). We shall consider this possibility later.

It will now be obvious that earlier descriptions of the acquisition of language owe much to a belief in an innate grammar. From McNeill's interpretations of Greenfield's analysis of holophrastic utterances to Braine's theory of pivot and open class words there was a general consensus that the earliest language behaviour was governed by grammatical rules. Whilst these explanations are often plausible they are difficult to verify. Indeed it is difficult to see how the empiricist can contribute to a better understanding of Chomsky's theory. It is impossible to examine competence, all raw data must be performance; and it is impossible to apply external criteria to utterances until intuition has been analysed adequately. This will not be easy. Native speakers may agree about the acceptability of many of Chomsky's sentences, but there may be many sentences about which there is disagreement. Much poetry may, by its unusual constructions and juxtaposing of unexpected words, belong in an intermediate area where intuitions of reliable native speakers do not agree.

A Piagetian Model

Piaget and his colleagues have been criticised for having paid too little attention to the function of language, both in their experiments and in its implications for their theory of intellectual functioning (Brown, 1981). Although there may be some degree of ambiguity, there is a frequently expressed opinion in theoretical papers by the Genevans that language only reflects the intellectual structures which have already been achieved. This is not to say that it may not have attentional functions or serve to keep an item in short term memory, but a child's language structure will only reflect relationships which the child is already capable of demonstrating non-linguistically (Inhelder and Sinclair, 1969).

Lunzer (1968) adopts Piagetian terminology in an attempt to match the data of psycholinguistics to the general area of intellectual development. He uses the term *strategy* to describe the operations which an individual may perform at any given time in order to regulate his behaviour; and the term *schema* to describe the pattern of interrelationships of various ideas which may be used in a strategy. The hierarchical nature of schemas and strategies, with some strategies being essential and others optimal, could be used to represent the manner in which linguistic transformations are made. The formation of schemas, by processes of assimilation and accommodation would correspond to deep structure in generative linguistics, and would provide internal representations of reality with which linguistic items must match. The gradual change of grammatical rules as the child develops would then be accounted for by the process of equilibration. Persistent use of the 'add *s*' for all plurals would be superseded when the results conflicted with the child's perceptions of the use of plurals by others. The resultant disequilibrium would lead to a restructuring of a more sophisticated schema.

One advantage of such a view is that it converts notions of deep structure into a terminology with which we are familiar in other areas of intellectual development. If the basis of deep structure is to be seen as an *experiential* rather than a linguistic phenomenon this might be a fruitful relationship.

Written Language

A great deal has been said about the development of speech, and it would seem logical now to examine the development of written language. In the past researchers seem to have afforded it scant attention, although it is now enjoying renewed interest (see Scardamalia, 1981, Wilkinson, 1985). It is frequently conceived as a second-order activity, being a visual form of utterances which the originator could make, although it is not a direct copy of speech. Comparison of transcribed speech and written words will show that for most people the two are dissimilar. Some consider it an alternative mode of expression rather than a second-order activity (Smith, 1973). It also requires an additional synthesis of sensory modes. Earler we spoke of the interrelationship of an object schema and a word schema (as a sound pattern). To this we must add a visual schema if the word is to be written or read.

The problems of perceptual discrimination have already been discussed (Chapter 3). Before the child can write or read he must be able to identify the symbols and the sounds they represent. Evidence suggests that visual recognition may be possible quite early, but that the association of the symbol with a sound, a cross-modal link between vision and auditory discrimination, may take longer. For written language the child must also have a high degree of motor coordination. Bruner (1975) has drawn attention to the importance of reading and writing. He suggested that the mind of a person who spent much of his time in these activities might be 'profoundly different' from that of one who was involved in non-linguistic activities such as drawing or building, and perhaps even different from that of one who mostly talked and listened. He suggested that there may be a minimal use of language in ordinary discourse which has little effect upon an individual's thought patterns, but beyond that level it may transform them. The most important step in this transformation he saw as instigated by the transference from speech into some form of notation such as writing or mathematical symbols. In this form it becomes more powerful. The rules which must be obeyed to construct written sentences may allow some people to analyse the products of their thoughts and to operate with formal operations (Piaget's term) in ways which would not otherwise be possible.

It has been observed that quite young children will make marks on a piece of paper. Many authorities feel that the infant's spoken language

Child development

and his attitude to the use of writing are very strongly influenced by the type of stimulation and encouragement he receives in the early years. Up to now we have discussed the child's approximations to a hypothetical adult language form. Now we need to examine the evidence for some fundamental differences in the ways people use their language.

Social Effects upon Language Acquisition

Bernstein (1971) puts forward a thesis that there is a very important difference in the quality of speech utterances used by members of the working class and of the middle class. The difference is thought to go far beyond variations of dialect or the use of slang and to be related to the actual function served by syntax and vocabulary. This linguistic class difference is said to be implicated in the overall perspective which each class has of the social system. Family settings, schools and work situations are seen as the main socialising agents through which these perspectives are acquired, and it is the first of these to which Bernstein and his associates have directed their attention.

Bernstein characterises the working class family as having an authority structure in which the status of the individual is clearly delineated. Analysis of their utterances is said to indicate a *restricted code*. Middle class families, it is suggested, pay more attention to the uniqueness of the individual, and this is shown in the *elaborated code* structure of their language.

A restricted code is defined as having narrow, rigid linguistic resources which make it difficult for the speaker to communicate his intent. It is rooted in the 'here and now' and is often only intelligible to participants in the situation, that is, it is *context-bound* and its meanings are *particularistic* or implicit.

The elaborated speech patterns of the middle class, on the other hand, are described as flexible and adaptable to convey meanings in a variety of forms. It is not restricted to an immediate situation but is *context-free*. Elaborated codes enable principles and operations to be made explicit, that is, the meanings are *universalistic*.

At a superficial level the two codes may be identified by certain linguistic differences, such as length of utterances, existence of simple and repetitive conjunctions such as 'so', 'then', quality and variety of adjectives used (see Bernstein, 1960).

This approach has given rise to much speculation concerning social class differences and their educational implications. If it is true that the language brought to school by the working class child is fundamentally different from that which middle class children *and teachers* use, then it represents a very serious communication problem for the teacher. Yet the thesis is not without its critics. Lawton (1968) commented that there was not the evidence to demonstrate that restriction at a linguistic level was necessarily followed by restriction in behavioural dimensions, Labov (1969) argued forcibly that his research into non-structured utterances of black Americans showed none of the deficits implied by Bernstein's theory, and Rosen (1972) criticised both the research methodology and the notion of two language forms. He suggested that a simple dichotomy of language functions, whilst elegant, did not adequately describe what he saw as a multiplicity of language forms of various qualities which proved more or less efficient in a wide variety of social situations.

The debate continues. With regard to the acquisition of language there is evidence from other sources that parents in the working class perceive their role somewhat differently from those in the middle class, and that they use different forms of exhortation and explanation to convey their expectations to their offspring (Hess and Shipman, 1965; Newson and Newson, 1970). Hess and Shipman's study of maternal control behaviours consisted of asking Negro mothers from middle and working class homes to teach their four-year-old children a block-sorting task. The children's success rates and the quality of mother-child interactions during teaching were recorded. Middle class mothers were found to motivate their children better, to establish an appropriate set, to give positive verbal reinforcement and specific instructions, and also to elicit verbal responses from their children.

There are a number of confirmatory studies in this area, (see Robinson, 1972). They have given rise to a popular idea which relates to Bernstein's work and which is well expressed by Hess and Shipman as 'the meaning of deprivation is the deprivation of meaning'. That is, working class children may suffer in their cognitive development because their parents use language forms which do not encourage exploratory behaviour and which do not accurately pin-point the meanings of the stimuli with which the children are confronted. Such fundamental differences might be expected to have repercussions in many aspects of the child's life, in his intellectual, social and emotional development.

Tizard (1974) urges caution with this assumption of a generalised disadvantage. She points out that there is no obvious causal relationship between the status of a man's job and his children's performance in school. Many children who have reading difficulty, and who may be assumed to suffer from inadequate verbal stimulation at home, may prove to have sufficient knowledge of language structure to become readers (Francis, 1974). Furthermore, Tizard cites Cole, Bruner and Bernstein in support of her contention that the 'failures' of working class children stem from an inability to transfer the skills they possess to the school-based situation, *and* from low motivation, not from absence of the skills in question.

Ryan (1974) has emphasised the consideration of other aspects of human interaction in addition to the linguistic competence of the individuals. One of these is the notion of *intersubjectivity*. At the beginning of this chapter reference was made to the possible shared meanings of 'John has a new wife'. The interpretation of that sentence was dependent upon the knowledge which speaker and listener brought to the situation. It will be recalled that Piaget's term *egocentric speech* was also used to describe a speech pattern uttered when no account had been taken of the listener's prior knowledge; that is, in the absence of adequate intersubjectivity.

Brown, Cazden and Bellugi observed that parents react to children's utterances in ways which provide amplified and corrected models. Long before this, however, the infant will be producing babbling which the parents are quite unable to identify; yet parents seem to believe, correctly or incorrectly, that the baby is trying to talk. Ryan suggests that a number of cues may be used to support this belief. Firstly, the interaction patterns may sound similar to those used by adults to express pleasure, enquiry, protest, etc.; secondly, the utterances may be accompanied by gesture or other activity; and finally the utterances may occur in the presence or absence of particular objects or people. Such considerations may lead parents to accept a sound as the infant's 'word' for something although it has no resemblance to the adult word.

In analyses of discourse between the parent and child the search for shared meaning is highlighted. Intersubjectivity is clearly as important a consideration as linguistic competence, yet until recently it has received little attention. To return to the utterance 'John has a new wife'. The meaning of this depends, not upon the sentence construction but upon the knowledge which speaker and listener share.

6

Personality and Social Development

The developmental process, which transforms the relatively helpless infant into the competent adult, is remarkable. Previous chapters have attempted to describe specific aspects of this process, linguistic and intellectual, yet it was clear that the chosen subdivisions were arbitrary. Developments in language will affect the child's intellectual abilities, and may have important implications for his interaction with friends. They are all aspects of an integrated system.

This chapter is concerned primarily with the development of more global features, which to some extent incorporate notions of perceptual, intellectual and linguistic change. These are the development of personality and social competence. Whilst some researchers concern themselves with specific mechanisms, others develop theories concerning the total changes which turn an *asocial* organism into a recognisable member of the human race.

Personality is a term which denotes a whole range of attributes which an individual may be said to possess and which are manifest in his modes of behaviour and thought. Its use presupposes that these modes are not random or unrelated, but are clustered together by virtue of certain observable characteristics which they have in common. That is to say, a person who is shy of social interaction is unlikely to be so only in one sort of situation, but may display similar shyness in a number of contexts, in interviews, at parties and dances, in shops and in interaction with teachers. It can be seen that personality is a complex concept which may involve his bodily functions, his emotional reactions, his social behaviour, his needs and desires, his attitudes, and his thinking processes.

Not surprisingly theories of personality and social development are diverse. William James (1890) started from a supposition the infants were totally unable to cope with the sensations which bombarded them

111

from within their bodies and from their surrounding environment; he described them as a 'blooming, buzzing confusion'. In his view the developing person acquired means of regulating and organising this confusion. Some of the early behaviourists took a similar view. To them the infant was a 'blank tablet of clay' on which regularities of the environment gradually impressed patterns by conditioning. Later behaviourists felt the need to assume some patterns or dispositions before conditioning took place. To them, the development of the person was the accumulation of conditioned responses, given that the infant had a tendency to attend to certain events more closely than to others.

Freud took a stronger nativist view, arguing that quite specific patterns of development were predetermined because the child went through a given sequence of stages, in each of which he was sensitive to different types of experience. Whilst the final product, the adult personality, would be formed by the quality of experience provided by the environment, the manner in which the person can attempt to deal with that experience was predetermined.

Because the child became sensitive to differing aspects of his environment, and because this was sometimes coupled with variations in his environment, Freud's theory can predict quite significant changes in personality during its development. Other authors have assumed fundamental *traits* which do not change much over time (Cattell, 1965; Eysenck, 1970). They suggest that the tendency to be out-going, friendly and sociable may be dependent upon innate mechanisms. In such theories the developmental aspect is limited to consideration of what are usually relatively superficial changes brought about by changes in the environment.

In this chapter some of the major developmental theories of personality will be reviewed. Consideration will then be given to social awareness, moral development, achievement seeking behaviour and the effects of maternal deprivation, areas of particular interest to many who are domestically or professionally concerned with children.

Psychoanalytic Theory

Sigmund Freud, the founder of psychoanalytic theory, viewed personality development as the result of genetically determined mechanisms interacting with the environment. The genetic mechanisms were common to all humans, but the environment would constrain the ways in which they could operate. Under favourable conditions the interaction of genetic and environmental factors would be reasonably harmonious, and would foster normal progression. Under unfavourable conditions, such as an excessively harsh environment, development could be arrested, or *fixated*. This would result in an abnormal adult personality.

Freud was a doctor. he worked in Vienna and was greatly influenced by two scientific fields which were making great advances at the turn of the century. One of these was embryology and the other energy dynamics. His 'unfolding' view of development is clearly similar to embryological notions, and Freud's description of *libido* or psychic energy and the ways in which it is employed by the personality may not be too unfamiliar to the physicist. These two formative influences impinged on Freud in a societal setting which we would think of as repressive or Victorian. Protocol and social niceties were strictly observed, sexual matters were never discussed openly, and even features such as table legs were sometimes draped so that the sight of them should not prompt unaccceptable thoughts. In the home the father was expected to dominate and to adopt a strong, forceful, 'masculine' role. Mothers were to administer to the needs of the husband and children, and to be gentle, docile and 'feminine'. Children were to be seen (when appropriate) but not heard. Clearly not all families behaved in this way, and we know from historical studies that the superficial puritanism belied considerable licentiousness. Nevertheless the fact that natural desires and inclinations had to be so carefully hidden in many families may have led Freud to emphasise the importance of sexual drives in his interpretation of human development.

According to Freud's theory (Brown, 1961) the driving force of the human psyche is the attainment of satisfaction and pleasure, principally through the gratification of sexual desires. Sexual desires, in this context, encompass not only physical sexuality but general physical sensuality and well-being also. The seat of this life-seeking instinct, and of its counterpart the death instinct, is the *id*, which is described as a seething cauldron of primitive impulses. When an impulse is manifest in the id the result is an immediate move toward gratification through fantasy, with no concern for the propriety of the act, not its rationality or legality. The id is driven solely by a 'Pleasure Principle'.

Growing directly out of the id in the earliest years of life is the *ego*. This is governed by the 'Reality Principle' and its purpose is to mediate between the instincts in the id and the external environment in order to determine acceptable means by which the instincts may be gratified.

Freud believed that dreams represented the fantasies of the id largely uncontrolled by the ego. They were, therefore, a valuable source of information for the psychiatrist.

Last to develop is the superego, which represents the idealistic aspect of the personality. It develops more slowly because it depends upon the acquisition of moral standards from the outside environment, principally from the parents. The superego also contains the *ego ideal*, or desirable self-image, against which the individual evaluates himself.

The human personality was seen by Freud as the resultant of complex interactions between the conflicts of the id, ego and superego. The matter is complicated further by the fact that they can operate at different levels. the id, for instance, is an unconscious phenomenon. That is, the individual is not aware of the impulses and tensions which exist in it. The ego, on the other hand, has a practical task to perform, and of necessity operates largely in the individual's consciousness, although part of it may be in the pre-conscious. This is an intermediate level of consciousness containing items of which the individual is not

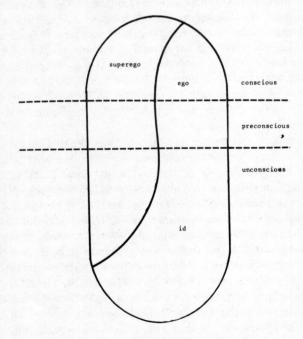

Figure 6.1 The Freudian model of the mind

immediately aware, but which he can uncover by his own mental efforts, unlike the unconscious which is only available through dreams or through the mediation of an analyst. The superego is also largely a conscious phenomenon, though it will contain some unconscious material. These levels are represented in Figure 6.1.

Human personality is made up of the structures described above, but their interaction with the environment will produce the outward manifestations of the personality which we normally use to characterise a person. To Freud this interaction was also highly structured. Throughout childhood the energy from the id's instincts is focussed first on one feature of the body, then on another, so that the child's personality will normally develop through a series of stages. These stages are more than transient phenomena, however, for the ease or difficulty with which the child progresses through a given stage will have a profound effect upon his adult personality.

The first year of life constitutes the *oral* stage of development. At this time the child is highly dependent upon his mother for survival. Gratification is achieved primarily from the lips and mouth, initially by sucking and chewing and later by biting. What is at first purely sensual, later develops into mechanisms which are capable not only of achieving physical gratification but of expressing aggression and inflicting pain. Adults who fail to pass through this stage satisfactorily are said to be showing *oral fixation*. Compulsive eating and certain forms of aggressive behaviour are described by psychoanalysts as examples of this.

During the second year of development, the *anal* stage, the focus of the sex drive is upon the anus and the process of defecation. At this time the parents are likely to be concerned with toilet training and the child discovers that whilst expulsion of faeces can be a pleasurable experience, retention may be used as a means of punishing parents. Excessive stress during this stage may lead to anal fixations which the adult may display as obsessional behaviour or sadism.

Between the third and fifth year the focus of the libido becomes the genitals. This is the *phallic* stage in which the child develops sexual attraction toward the opposite-sex parent. It was considered an important stage because the differences between the sexes during this period provided a base upon which later sex identities depend. In a boy the emergence of sexual desire for the mother leads to hostility towards the father and to fear that he will castrate him. Normal development results in the resolution of this 'Oedipal' conflict by the boy identifying strongly with the father. Thus by 'becoming' the father the boy can to some extent 'possess' the mother. The process of identification builds the superego and determines the direction of adolescent sex-typing. Sexual desire for the mother is also experienced by girls, although it is inhibited by anxiety because the girl has no penis. The girl's *penis envy* was seen by Freud as part of the hapless situation of the female from which there was no ultimately satisfying resolution. The girl felt that she was already punished by castration. Subsequently a daughter will transfer her desire to her father from whom she desires a child and/or the return of the penis (the two being equated in the girl's mind). Partial resolution is possible by identification with the mother but the superego's morality was considered less robust than that of the boy.

Freud said very little about the period from about the age of six to the age of puberty. He termed this the *latency* period and suggested that it was largely a period of consolidation and of developing skills and knowledge. Psycho-sexual considerations were in abeyance, the urges being inhibited during the resolution of the Oedipal complex.

Finally genetic forces re-emerged at puberty. Once again the individual showed much of the aggressive, egocentric behaviour of the infant, as these forces overpowered the individual's ability to inhibit his urges. This was the *genital* stage, characterised by the acquisition of adult heterosexuality and the relinquishing of parental ties.

Since Freud developed his theory there have been many who, whilst working within the general framework, have wished to change the emphasis. In particular there has been increased emphasis on interaction with the environment and less upon the genetically determined psycho-sexual drives. Melanie Klein (1932) is typical of this trend. Erikson (1950) put forward a theory of 'developmental tasks of childhood' which had a similar emphasis, and which embellished the somewhat vague and insubstantial descriptions of the latency period. Blos (1962) used Kleinian notions in his analyses of adolescence. He also emphasised the positive attributes of regression or reverting to an earlier form of behaviour, which enabled the adolescent to recapitulate and adjust unsatisfactory aspects of former stages, at the same time preparing to sever the bonds with the parent and form new adult heterosexual bonds.

To the developmental psychologist psychoanalytic theory is of great historical significance. The concept of identification has even been taken up by social behaviourists (see below). Yet psychoanalytic notions do not really meet the requirements of a scientific theory, for they are not refutable. In many instances mechanisms are described which give rise to certain behaviours and it might be assumed that these causal relationships could be tested, except that in certain circumstances the absolute opposite form of behaviour may be displayed. For instance the theory might explain why a child would fear his father. If the prediction is contested by evidence that this child protests and displays love for the father, this can be explained as a process of reaction formation as defence against an unconscious fear. Problems of this kind have led to the assertion that psychoanalytic theory lacks utility as it is 'unsinkable'. The importance of the possibility of refutation in science has been extensively explained by Popper (1974). Nevertheless Kline (1981) maintains that there is acceptable scientific evidence for many of Freud's notions, though the argument is contested by Eysenck and Wilson (1973).

Nevertheless, Freud has made important contributions to psychological thought. His emphasis upon learning in infancy and its effects upon the adult personality is one which is widely accepted. Furthermore, his descriptions of these learning processes were frequently in terms of the relationships between infants and their parents, giving rise to an interest in the dynamic aspects of human interaction. His studies of dreams and the defence mechanisms, by which the individual protected himself, drew attention to the idea that much of the mind may operate at an unconscious level. It is an interesting conjecture that very few contemporary psychologists would deny the possibility, even probability, of unconscious processes; yet hardly any of them research this area.

Social Learning Theory

Trait theories are concerned with discovering the inborn attributes which make up an individual's personality. Psychoanalytic theory, in its original form, also leans very heavily upon inherited factors. The actual amount of libido which a person possesses, and the manner in which it is focused first on one object then another are not considered susceptible to cultural or class influences. Another group of theorists took a different approach, or more accurately a number of approaches. These are called the Social Learning Theorists, and their work changes the emphasis from that of Freud, with its invariant cycle of mechanisms which interacted with the environment, to one in which only simple, physiological drives are seen as innate.

Their basic model is derived from the notions of conditioning, and proposes that people acquire *habits* by learning to respond in specific ways to specific stimuli. The impetus to develop habits stems in the first place from the basic physiological drives, usually those listed as examples are hunger, thirst, respiration and sex (although it is arguable that the latter is different in almost every respect from those in which deprivation causes rapid and fatal deterioration of the organism). To the extent that early learning depends upon these *primary drives* the theory is nativist; but learning permits the development of secondary drives such as ambition or anxiety which motivate the learner when he is physiologically secure. It is with the acquisition of these secondary drives that these theories are primarily concerned. Whenever a response is made to a stimulus with a resulting drop in drive level there will be a tendency for a habit to develop. Frequent repetition of response will lead to its becoming a consistent part of the organism's behavioural repertoire. If the circumstances change, so that the response no longer causes reduction of the drive state, the habit will become weakened or may disappear altogether.

Dollard and Miller (1950) suggested that it was the acquisition of habits in infancy which were of paramount importance in forming personality. In particular habits relating to feeding, toilet training, early sex training and self-control of sexual and aggressive urges were stressed. It will be noted that these foci are precisely those involved in Freudian theory. The behaviourist model is less rigid than it might at first appear because of the concept of *generalisation*. By this process specific responses can be elicited not only from the stimulus with which they were first paired, but from others with some degree of similarity. For example, an infant may be motivated by hunger pains which are reduced when the breast is presented by his mother. The presence of mother will come to be associated with the warm, comfortable feeling produced by milk. Subsequently the feeling may be generalised to all adults with whom he comes into contact. This might be seen as a satisfactory state of affairs for an infant, but not for an old child. At a later stage adults may begin to punish the child for inappropriately familiar reactions to strange adults. A reverse process of *discrimination* learning is then being employed.

Kagan (1969) identifies four basic mechanisms in socialisation, a process which he describes as including the acquisition of social and intellectual skills, the elimination of undesirable behaviours and values, and the acquisition of desirable behaviours and values. These four mechanisms are (1) a desire for affection and acceptance, (2) a need to

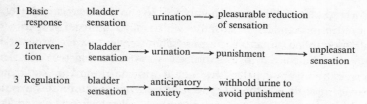

Figure 6.2 A behaviourist interpretation of the function of anxiety

avoid punishment or rejection, (3) a process of identification with particular people, and (4) a tendency to imitate. Kagan believes that these mechanisms are each important at different times in childhood, although they all involve 'inhibition of a behaviour that is relatively strong in the child's repertoire'. The first two mechanisms are general descriptions of drive states, either primary or secondary. These he embellishes by introducing *anxiety* as an anticipation of punishment, leading to internal regulation of behaviour (figure 6.2).

The author maintains that the emotion of anxiety always has a cognitive aspect, and this enables the child to relate it to specific bodily functions or unaccepted behaviours. In early childhood, but not in infancy, the main sources of anxiety are thought to be potential loss of maintenance of affection, anticipation of physical harm, and dissimilarity between the child's beliefs and behaviours and those accepted by society.

Previously we considered identification as a psychoanalytic concept, but reference was made to its use by behaviourists. In this context it refers to a process in which the child perceives some similarities with another person. If the child also recognises certain rewards or punishments which he believes the model to be experiencing he too may experience some pleasureable feelings, as though he had been reinforced and will progressively adopt habits similar to the model's. Maccoby (1959) and Kagan (1969) see the initial stage of this process as imitation, a disposition to copy, and the second stage as being identification, whereas Bronfenbrenner (1960) queries the existence of this general imitative motive and Bandura (1962) considers both to be part of a single process in which the characteristics of the model and exposure to them are all that is involved in what he terms identification. No reference is made in these studies to the initial level of perceived similarity.

Bandura and his co-workers (Bandura, Ross and Ross, 1963a, 1963b) observed that children were highly selective in the models with which they identified and in the attributes which they acquired. In experimentally controlled situations nursery school children were exposed to adults who behaved in pre-arranged ways indicating that they had power or no power, that they could provide reward or could not provide reward, and then they were or were not nurturant towards the child. In the course of performing certain tasks the adults would also accomplish certain irrelevant acts such as putting on peculiar articles of clothing or shouting.

When asked to perform the tasks themselves the children tended to imitate some of the irrelevant acts too. The researchers found the children to be more influenced by adults who wielded power, who provided reward, and who were nurturant than those they perceived to be in similar situations to themselves. They also tended to adopt aggressive behaviours shown by adults, particularly if they had led to rewards rather than punishment.

Then identification process was found to be exceedingly complex, however. Whilst general characteristics of the most likely sources of modelling were delineated, it is not always possible to determine which behavioural attributes the children would copy. Furthermore there was indication of some sex differences. Male power figures were more potent than females, and in situations in which the female model failed to reward a male, boys identified more with the deprived male than the powerful female. It is this evidence which led Kagan (1969) to emphasise a preliminary stage of perceived similarity before further identification takes place. He argues that if a child feels that he shares no attributes with the model he is unlikely to derive vicarious reinforcement from the model's successes.

Perhaps the best documented emotional reaction in the behaviourist tradition is fear. Watson and Raynor (1920) demonstrated that a young child could be conditioned to fear a white rat, to which he had shown no fear previously. This was accomplished by pairing presentations of the white rat with a loud and startling clash of metal. After only a few such pairings the rat alone evoked a fear response in the child, and this quickly generalised to other furry animals such as rabbits.

That emotional reactions can be learned is undeniable. They are also extremely persistent. It is now more than forty years since the writer experienced air raids, yet a recent recording of the alert siren on the television and within the comfort of his own peaceful lounge, was sufficient to bring the tense, anxious physical reactions back.

Happily, what can be learned can be unlearned, or more specifically a new response can be substituted for the old one. By pairing presentations of a feared animal with the presentation of sweets Jones (1924) was able to replace a fear reaction with one of pleasure.

Role Theory

Another method of describing the development of the person is in terms of role theory. This is sometimes described rather crudely as a theory which propounds the view that every person in a society has to play a number of roles, such as son, brother, pupil, friend, etc., and that society has defined the permissible limits of these roles in terms of behaviours which are mandatory, others which are optional and others which are proscribed. The process of socialisation then becomes one of learning these definitions and acquiring habits which are compatible with them. Descriptions of this sort do not adequately portray contemporary role theory however. Such a simplified view does not account for the fact that individuals fill the same role in remarkably different ways, or that it is difficult to specify role definitions, even within relatively homogeneous subcultures.

A more elaborate version (Turner, 1969) differentiates between the *enacted role*, which an unbiased observer may perceive the individual to be acting out, and the *perceived role*, as seen by the actor himself. The latter is a product of the individual's own mental process, a concept formation of tasks from what he sees as relevant data in his experience. This emphasis provides a looser frame of reference, made even more idiosyncratic when it is realised that, whatever the actor's perceived role, it may not match very closely his enacted role. For example, the author of this text may or may not share with the reader a fairly clear definition of the role of a textbook author. Alas, even if he does, the author's enacted role...

Perhaps the most crucial role which the child must attain is the sex-role. Failure to adopt socially acceptable behaviours can lead to conflict and ostracism quite early in childhood, and subsequently to possible unhappiness and maladjustment. Anthropological studies suggest that our stereotypes of masculine or feminine behaviour are very heavily influenced by cultural factors, and behaviour which would cause a boy or man to be labelled effeminate in one society may be perfectly normal in another. Margaret Mead (1949) gave fascinating evidence to this effect in her accounts of the child-rearing patterns in New Guinea.

Cultural stereotypes pervade many aspects of society. At the face-to-face level parents controlling exhortations may subtly differ without their knowledge. If a brother strikes his sister he may be told 'Boys don't hit girls', yet when the tables are turned the daughter is told 'Girls don't fight' (see Sears, Maccoby and Levin, 1957 for a detailed discussion). On television construction sets are most frequently seen in the hands of boys and dolls and nurses sets being played with by girls. It may be argued that this simply reflects the present market trend, but it also serves as a source of data from which the child will determine the relevant sex-role behaviours. Similarly in school it has hitherto been customary for boys to study woodwork and metalwork and the girls to study domestic science and needlework. In mixed secondary schools an unrepresentatively low proportion of girls enter the sixth form science classes and even fewer the computer clubs. There is a distinct possibility that in contemporary society these sex-typed attitudes may be changing. Schools are offering greater freedom for children to participate in studies previously reserved for the other sex. A highly articulate campaign for the reappraisal of women's rights and opportunities is making its presence felt in the wider society. It will be interesting to see whether these counter-stereotype trends have much effect upon children before any changes are seen in the opinions of the majority of adults. It now seems that the changes will occur more slowly than had previously been hoped.

Not only do sex roles differ between cultures, but also the ways in which sexuality and sexual behaviour are regarded can vary considerably. Malinowski (1927) and Mead (1962) reported societies in which normal sexual relationships within the tribe were openly acknowledged, and in which sexually maturing adolescents were not expected to deny thier impulses. For this reason the transition from childhood to adult status was made without apparent difficulty. Evidence from many sources now suggests that it is incorrect to regard adolescence as automatically involving emotional tension and stress. Where it exists it is the result of pressures placed upon the emergent adult by the demands of the culture. In Britain and America education is prolonged and school denotes immaturity to many people. Not only do we depend on extensive apprenticeship for adult status, we also fail to initiate the adolescent into many essential skills. We provide little guidance in sexual matters and we provide schooling which frequently bears little relationship to the individual's future career. '... adolescents are in the position of knowing that it is important for them to get somewhere in a hurry, but they know only roughly where, and have an even poorer idea of how to proceed' (Mussen, Conger and Kagan, 1963). Nevertheless all western adolescents are by no means emotionally unstable. The 'storm and stress' view propagated by Neo-Freudians (see Gustin, 1961; Hall, 1904) has been much criticised (Bandura, 1964). It is probably more accurate to say that adolescence represents a time of *role transition* (Elder, 1968) and at such times the individual is always prone to emotional disturbance. It can be obviated, however, if the social situation clearly delineates the requirements of the new role, and if maturer colleagues are tolerant and supportive during the transition period.

Theories in Perspective

The preceding theories share some common ground. Indeed it would be very surprising if they did not, for they are all attempts to explain the same thing; how the new-born child develops into a person. To put them in perspective it might help to see how each theory might attempt to explain the anxiety of a five-year-old child.

To psychoanalysts, toilet training is an activity which frequently arouses anxiety which may persist, in some form or another, for a lifetime. During the second year of life (the anal stage) parents may over-emphasise cleanliness and may punish the child for failing to produce faeces at the appropriate time, and in the appropriate receptacle. The act of defecation thus becomes fraught with tension, yet at the same time the child gets physical pleasure from the expulsion of faeces. This conflict of pleasure and fear may lead to the development of anxiety associated with ambiguous feelings toward the parents, or adults in general. To alleviate the situation the child would need to understand the cause of his anxiety and reassess his relationships with his parents.

A behaviourist sees anxiety as an anticipatory internal response. He may also look to toilet training as the event which precipitated it, but his explanation of the underlying mechanism would be different. During severe toilet training the mother may withdraw affection as a means of coercing the child. She may look angry, refuse to talk to the child, or may refuse his affection. 'Presence of mother' and 'fear' then become associated by the child. The unpleasantness of this situation may be anticipated when next the child considers approaching the mother, causing anticipatory anxiety. Subsequently the child may generalise the response to all adult authority figures, and the anticipation of

CD-I

permanent control in a classroom may lead to continuous anxiety.

The explanation may not seem very different, but the treatment would be. Any conditioned response can be eliminated and another put in its place. By ensuring that a substantial proportion of contacts with adults were reinforcing, perhaps involving rewards such as overt affection or sweets, a new association of 'adult' and 'pleasure' could be established.

Role theory would seek explanation in the situation in which the child perceived himself. At the age of five he may have entered school, and may perceive the expectations as very different from those he was accustomed to playing. If the parents were very indulgent, allowing the child to behave in any way he chose, yet sheltering him from potentially difficult or problematic situations, he may experience a difficult role transition to that of a pupil, sharing teacher with thirty other children, restricted in his behaviours, and frequently presented with difficult tasks.

Successful role adoption depends upon the individual's ability to accommodate change, and upon the degree of change demanded. The anxiety of the five-year-old may be allayed, if it is imaginary, by demonstrating that expectations are not what he perceives. If they are real, parents and teachers should attempt to modify their expectations so that the role transition is not abrupt. Many experienced teachers do this, by adapting their demands to the perceived competence of the individual pupil.

An interesting version of an interaction between hereditary and environmental factors is proposed by Mischel (1976) who suggests that it might be profitable to conceive of behaviour as resulting from hereditary personality traits functioning in settings which exhibit differing degrees of constraint. Places such as examination rooms and orchestral concert halls are, by consensus, environments in which there is little opportunity for individual variations in behaviour to be manifest. Hence the extravert and the introvert may be obliged to respond in very similar fashion. A garden fete, on the other hand, permits of a wide variety of acceptable behaviours, and the introvert may well seek a secluded spot to read his book and to escape the extravagant behaviour of his more extraverted colleague.

Developing Social Awareness

Unlike the young of some other animals, the human infant cannot support its own life. Food and warmth must be provided for it. Therefore humans can only exist as *social* beings in the early stages of life, though they may subsequently opt for total independence or even isolation. Newson (1974) suggests that the inanimate environment is very poor stimulation for a baby, and that it is the influence of other humans with power to communicate and 'tune in' to the baby's behaviours and interests, which are vital in developing the shared meanings of the world which we call knowledge.

Trevarthen (1975) takes a nativist view of this interaction process. He believes that behaviour is biologically organised into timed episodes which are potential gestures, in which various motor activities are fully synchronised. The episodes last for only a second or two, and are only perceptible by slow-motion videotaped recording, but they are of the same temporal pattern as that used by all humans. Trevarthen calls the activity *pre-speech*.

The possible presence of pre-speech does not necessarily imply any intention to communicate on the part of the infant. All that is necessary is a pre-programmed mechanism which emits behaviour in characteristically human episodes. It may be these which dispose adults to see the baby as a human being, and to ascribe to him all the capacities of thought and feeling which they themselves possess. Prolonged exposure to adult ministrations will lead to the development of new skills which enable the baby to demand and reward attention, in other words to genuine interaction between persons. Until quite recently there was a widespread belief that these processes were probably characteristic of the whole human species. However there is now evidence of marked cultural differences (Kaye, 1984).

With whom the child interacts, and in what manner, is not only dependent on the foregoing behaviours of course. Contemporary researchers are discovering many capacities which were hitherto unsuspected, because there was no substantial activity to be seen (c.f. Bower, 1974). Yet clearly mobility and physical capacities are important, and whilst there may be no fundamental reason why a new-born infant could not interact with peers, the chances are that such interaction will not occur for a year or two. A much older tradition in child psychology has been concerned with the stages of interaction which are displayed in play patterns. Parten (1932) used the following widely accepted classification:

unoccupied: no obvious activity (note that contemporary psychologists using more sophisticated techniques would query the appropriateness of this heading).

onlooker: the child observes the activity of other children.

solitary play: plays alone.

parallel play: the child plays in the company of others, but there is little interaction.

associative play: the child plays with others, often adopting the same play activities and sharing materials, e.g. all the children decide to play with bricks.

cooperative play: the children collaborate and take on different but related tasks to further a common aim, e.g. roles of mother, father, policeman, are allocated in order to act out an incident.

Such a sequence has many contributing factors. Mobility, autonomy from parental supervision and linguistic ability are inter-related with developing skills to encourage or discourage the behaviours of others, to alienate or ally peers, and to acquire or retain necessary playthings. Furthermore, Parten did not find that older children totally abandoned solitary play, but that increasingly the more sophisticated patterns took up more of the total time (Figure 6.3).

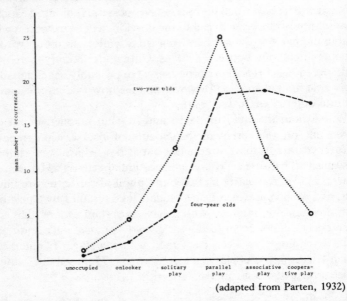

(adapted from Parten, 1932)

Figure 6.3 Comparison of play behaviours in two-year-old and four-year-old children

Charlesworth and Hartup (1967) adopted the categories described by the behaviourist, Skinner (1953), in an analysis of the methods employed by three- and four-year-olds to manipulate peers and establish preferred play patterns. The categories of reinforcement were (i) giving attention and approval, (ii) giving affection and personal acceptance, (iii) submission (passive acceptance of opinions and ideas, willingness to compromise (iv) token giving (spontaneous gift of toy, sweet etc.) Careful observation over several hours activity in the playgroup led the authors to conclude that most of this reinforcement occurred during those parts of the day set aside for dramatic (cooperative) play, and that the frequency of usage was directly related to age and sex, with older children, particularly boys, reinforcing most often.

It is important to remember that interaction is a two-way process. Each child learns to shape the behaviours of others, but is himself shaped by them. Some aspects of his personality may not be amenable to shaping, but very many more are open to modification. This does not imply that the individual is simply the product of environmental forces, for different children may have different susceptibilities to change. For example, two siblings may be brought up in a warm, open family setting which encourages humour, openness and out-going, sociable behaviour. Both children may be more out-going than they would have been in a different setting. Yet one child may be seen to be much more extravert than the other. This may be because the two children had different genetic predispositions to extraversion. Escalona (1969) put forward the view that children have different degrees of sensitivity in interaction. In a study of thirty-two infants over the period from four to thirty-two weeks she reported that those identified as active were more intensely excited by hunger and by social stimulation, whereas inactive infants indulged in more tactile and visual exploration, and were more stimulated by objects. Whilst querying the appropriateness of such a global view of sensitivity, Schaffer (1971), nevertheless, cites sufficient evidence for him to conclude 'there are marked individual differences in behavioural and autonomic reactivity to stimulation'.

Moral Development

The cultural differences which affect the acquisition of sex roles have already been discussed. These differences are a small part of the standards of conduct which societies develop to control the behaviour of their members. These moral codes may differ widely, yet no society however primitive, exists without them. It is difficult to define precisely what is meant by a moral code, but usually it involves the manner in which an individual behaves with respect to his fellow men. Typically it will include prescriptions of conduct concerning property, sexual behaviour and the resolution of interpersonal conflicts. Moral codes are deeply embedded in the beliefs of a culture, so that members will often declare that they 'know' that they 'should' behave in a certain way, but are unable to justify that belief.

The Psychoanalytic View of Morality

In Freudian theory the superego serves two functions, as a prescription of what the ideal self *should* do (the ego ideal), and as a prohibiting conscience which punishes transgressions by guilt (the conscience). Post-Freudians have tended to treat the two separately, reserving the term superego for the latter. Freud did not make this distinction, but his emphasis was upon guilt and its capacity to obstruct transgression.

During the Phallic stage of development the process of identification is intensified, with boys exhibiting special interest in their father as an ideal. The relationship with the mother also changes, as the boy seeks to possess her, an object relationship. This situation has its roots in an earlier phase of development but reaches its ultimate expression in the form of the Oedipus situation during the Phallic phase. Fear of castration by the father as punishment for desiring the mother can only be resolved by increased indentification with the father, thereby vicariously possessing the mother through the father's possession of her. The intense identification with the father is ambivalent, containing both love and hate for the anxiety the boy has suffered.

The female situation is necessarily rather different. Anxiety arises from penis envy because the girl feels that she has already been castrated. As an existing state of affairs Freud considered this less of a threat than that of castration anxiety. Identification is here with the mother, and an object relationship is established with the father.

The ideal resolution of the Oedipus situation is for the authority of the parent to be absorbed into the ego where it forms the nucleus for the superego. External punishment from the parent then becomes transformed into self-punishment in the form of guilt. Because of the more threatening aspect of the male Oedipal situation Freud believed males to possess stronger supergos than females, and to feel guilt more severely.

The development and functioning of the superego is more complex than this simplified account. In particular values and prohibitions absorbed by the individual will be in the highly subjective forms in which they are perceived. For this reason prediction of an individual's moral behaviour is very difficult.

Behaviourist Interpretations of Morality

Mowrer (1960) based his interpretation upon the process of imitation. Imitation which may initially be reinforced by adults may subsequently become rewarding in its own right. Vicarious reinforcement may also operate. That is, not only may a child observe an adult behaving in a certain way, but he may also witness him being rewarded. Empathy may dispose the child to behave in a similar way.

In addition, punishment which follows a forbidden behaviour will arouse an anxiety state in the child. This state will become associated with the situation which stimulated the forbidden behaviour, and may be sufficiently strong to prevent the behaviour being elicited. The child will build up a conditioned anticipatory mechanism (anxiety) which controls his own behaviour. In Mowrer's view this is what we call morality.

Because of a lack of relationship between moral behaviours in different situations, some authors have assumed that this interpretation must be invalid (Lovell, 1968). This is not necessarily so. It certainly weakens the argument because the rather sweeping claims for generalisation of conditioned responses is placed in doubt, but it does not invalidate the possibility that a basic conditioning situation might exist.

The Developmental Theories of Piaget and Kohlberg

Piaget (1932) investigated children's use of rules and views of justice. For the former he scrutinised the ways in which rules were used in the game of marbles.

Children below the age of six showed little conscious awareness of any rules. Even those which they acknowledged did not seem to constrain their behaviour in any way. The following six years were characterised by increasing *heteronomy*. Rules are fixed by others, probably adults; they are sacred and immutable. Whilst they contrain behaviour within a given situation they will not change a child's conduct in other situations for he is not aware of the meaning of the rule, only its application.

Subsequently rules are seen as compacts between individuals, for the purpose of fostering cooperation and reciprocity. They are now negotiable, but essential for a purpose. They are *autonomous*.

A similar development was seen in children's views of justice. Piaget asked them what should be done in a number of hypothetical situations involving other children's wrongdoings. Analysis of the replies suggested that, parallel with the development of autonomy, was a view of justice which changed from *realism* to *relativism*. During the early and middle parts of childhood the fixed, heteronemous rules coincided with a concept of justice which equated the seriousness of a misdemeanour with the extent of the outcome or the severity of the punishment incurred. A child who accidentally broke ten plates would have committed a more serious crime than one who deliberately smashed a single plate, or an act which merited a smack must be more serious than one which brought only a scolding. What was lacking was any concept of intent. Gradually this gave way to relativism in which the child was able to consider mitigating circumstances.

Punishments too, tend to be seen differently as the child gets older. Heteronemous rules are seen as involving punishments which inflict suffering in order to coerce obedience (*expiatory*). As rules acquire genuine, internalised meanings punishment also is revised. Whilst it may still involve suffering, this is a secondary consideration to the re-establishment of bonds of solidarity and reciprocity which rules represent (*reciprocal*).

	RULES	JUSTICE	PUNISHMENT
6 years	heteronemous	realistic	expiatory
10 years	autonomous	relativistic	reciprocal

It may seem that the description of morality given here is rather sophisticated for a secondary school child. Indeed most adults do not consistently behave in a way which is clearly influenced by an autonomous, relativistic and reciprocal morality. If, even in very general terms, the description is accurate, it would imply that morality involved conscious, logical processes. Bull (1969) made the point that actions and words often do not correspond. Piaget may well have obtained the children's statements about what they believed, but their behaviours may not be compatible with their beliefs. If this is so, then it would be possible for behaviour to be conditioned by earlier experiences, and for it to be unrelated to verbal responses to hypothetical situations.

Kohlberg (1964) has produced an extension of Piaget's work using very similar techniques. The results of his analyses suggest six developmental stages in morality, two at each of three levels. *Premoral level* (I) contained two stages characterised by the view that cultural rules and evaluative labels denote pleasant and unpleasant consequences, or reflect the influence of those who wield the power. Level II is described as *Conventional Role Conformity*, in which the child actively maintains the expectations of family and friends as values in their own right. Level III, *Self-Accepted Moral Principles* is concerned with defining moral values and principles without recourse to the authority of those imposing them, but in terms of the contractual obligations or basic human principles which all individuals must observe.

Respondents will typically give a variety of responses at various levels, but usually one level will predominate. Development is portrayed as a gradual diminution in the number of lower level responses and a complementary increase in those at a higher level, although Stage 6 (the latter half of Level III) is often not reached.

Kohlberg takes the view that it is not possible for respondents to fake in these procedures, for if an individual hears other possible answers which are preferable to his own he will adopt them as his own. However, it is unusual for this to occur if the alternative responses are more than one level above his own.

There are a number of studies which suggest that moral behaviour may be situation-specific, in the sense that a child may be honest in games situations and dishonest in his schoolwork. This need not negate the idea of a developmental trend. The manner in which he construes the games situation, and the reasons for his honesty may still show an organised progression. Similarly the frequently observed relationships between intelligence and morality (Graham, 1972) need not be seen as implying that brighter children are more honest, but only that their stated *reasons* for their behaviour were judged by the investigator to be superior. It is important to note that measures of morality usually assess sophistication of interpretation, not proportions of moral and immoral behaviour.

Achievement Motivation

Societies differ extensively in the amount of emphasis that is placed upon the ability of individuals publicly to demonstrate their skills, the extent to which the social order allows the competencies of one individual to be compared with another and the level of approbation which such demonstrations merit. Schools in the USSR tend to emphasise collective responsibility and the achievements of the group. Conformity, rather than the exercise of individuality, is what society expects (see Bronfenbrenner, 1972; Grant, 1964). In contrast school-children in Britain and America are frequently encouraged to compete with peers in order to demonstrate their superiority. Excellence can be achieved without comparison, yet the need to demonstrate excellence by attaining accepted public standards is intimately woven into the fabric of western societies. This need to achieve, often written as 'n' Ach, has been extensively studied over the past forty years. Smith (1969) lists the following as the factors which will determine an individual's performance in a task involving attainment of a standard of excellence; the motive to achieve, anxiety and the motive to avoid failure, the likelihood of success as perceived by the individual and the incentive value of reward.

McClelland (1958) developed the first instrument for measuring 'n' *Ach*. It consisted of a series of pictures derived from a projective test by Murray. A projective test is one which uses ambiguous or poorly defined stimuli, usually pictures, into which the subject 'projects' his own meaning. It is believed that in the absence of any real or objective meaning the content of the subject's description may relate to his own conscious or subconscious motives. McClelland devised a complex scoring system which enabled him to determine the amount of achievement motive in individuals.

Initially J.W. Atkinson worked with McClelland, but later they worked independently. Their views are somewhat different, McClelland seeing 'n' Ach as a motivational state which is greatly influenced by the task situation, Atkinson interpreting it more as a personality trait and ascribing variations in performance to expectations of success, the incentive of the goal, and the strength of a motive to avoid failure (Atkinson, 1964). Other workers have examined the antecedent conditions which might lead to differences in the level of 'n' Ach acquired by children, and it is with this developmental aspect we are primarily concerned.

Many factors such as social class, intelligence and parental influence have been implicated as antecedents of high or low achievement motivation. As social class and intelligence are related, and it seems likely that they operate as indices of actual parental behaviours anyway, we shall concentrate on the latter.

Kahl's well-known study of 'Common Man' (1953) reported that, in a sample of working class boys in high school those whose fathers accepted their lot and were concerned only to 'get by' had sons of similar disposition. Fathers who emphasised 'getting ahead' had achievement-oriented sons. Unfortunately the evidence was somewhat anecdotal and the study revealed nothing of the dynamics by which the disposition was passed on.

Lewin (1952) sought to distinguish parents whose restrictive attitudes were confined to setting acceptable limits for behaviour, whilst still encouraging the child to engage freely in activities within these limits, and those who issued imprecise cautions and warnings which inhibited any new behaviour. Similar views were expressed by McClelland *et al* (1953) and Winterbottom (1958).

Studies conducted at the Fels Research Institute (Crandall *et al*, 1960) reported that children's achievements in nursery school free-play were unrelated to maternal affection or reward of dependency-seeking behaviours, but positively related to reward of approval-seeking and achievement efforts. Subsequently Crandall suggested some sex differences with mother-daughter relationships being the most potent, but Katkovsky *et al* (1964a, 1964b) suggested that mother-son and father-daughter relationships were strongest.

Rosen and D'Andrade (1959) possibly presented the most succinct picture of parental involvement in achievement training. Children from forty families were selected on the basis of high or low 'n' Ach. Five experimental tasks were then set up in the home in the presence of the parents. High achievement oriented parents set high expectations for their children, estimated their competence as high and inspired standards of excellence in tasks where none was explicit. They expected the child to be independent and self-reliant and to accept responsibility for his own action. Demands for self-reliance in sons came from fathers. The mothers tended to be dominant and to expect less self-reliance. The authors suggested that the mother-son relationships were more secure and could withstand greater parental dominance without adversely affecting the son's 'n' Ach level.

There is a great deal of evidence that parental behaviour is implicated in the achievement motive of the developing child. Yet in many studies the effects, whilst remarkably strong, leave much to be accounted for. Featherman (1972) concluded that one could not support the view that 'n' Ach measures were highly relevant to education until some attempt had been made to define these 'other factors'.

Attribution Theory

Stemming from 'n' Ach studies, but rapidly developing into a major field in its own right, is attribution theory. At its simplest level it involves investigation of what individuals perceive as the causes of their own successes and failures. A burgeoning literature in the last two decades suggests that, whilst there is a number of influential factors which may intervene, the basic tendency is for people to attribute results either to their own capabilities or to the effects of outside influences. Furthermore, these dispositions seem to be relatively stable (Weiner, 1980).

Early studies demonstrated that when children were asked to explain their performances on a variety of tasks of varying degrees of difficulty, they tended to do so in terms of what Heider (1958) called *personal qualities* or *environmental factors*; and what Rotter (1966) subsequently described as *internal* or *external locii of control*. These different attributions might be signified respectively by "I'm hopeless at maths" and "He gave us a really hard maths test". Heider went on to introduce another variable into the equation, the extent to which factors fluctuated over time. These possibilities can be represented as:

	STABLE	UNSTABLE
INTERNAL	ability	effort
EXTERNAL	task difficulty	luck

Clearly, the belief that one is "hopeless at maths" implies a relatively stable feature, but whether "He gave us a really hard test" implies stability (because the test will not alter) or instability (because it was unlucky that he selected that one) is certainly not so clear.

Such problems of definition led to further elaboration of the model, in which attempts were made to implicate intentions into the theory. The table from Rosenbaum (1972) illustrates this. (fig. 6.4)

Evidence indicated the not surprising conclusion that when an individual assesses his ability or degree of effort he does so by comparing himself with other people. But the human capacity to handle information is distinctly limited as we have seen, so estimates made by people

	INTENTIONAL		UNINTENTIONAL	
	STABLE	UNSTABLE	STABLE	UNSTABLE
INTERNAL	stable effort of self	unstable effort of self	ability of self	fatigue, mood or fluctuation in skill
EXTERNAL	stable effort of others	unstable effort of others	ability of others or task difficult	fatigue, mood or fluctuations in skill of others or luck

(Rosenbaum, 1972; cited by Weiner, 1974)

Figure 6.4 Rosenbaum's model of attributions

are unlikely to be entirely rational. If, in a series of performances with varying degrees of success, the earlier efforts prove to be relatively good, people tend to over-estimate their ability, and *vice versa*.

There is also reluctance on the part of a great many people to accept that events may occur at random. So causal relationships may be assumed where none exist. It may be this human failing which accounts for the well-proven rule that it always rains when the car has just been cleaned.

Smith (1978) has suggested that young children are susceptible to attributing intention to many accidental acts performed by others, particularly if the consequences are severe. This, in fact, is a restatement in attributional terms of some of Piaget's findings (see p. 129).

In the past decade studies have investigated many aspects of child motivation using attribution theory. It has been proposed that the extent to which parents coerce their children into compliant behaviour may influence the children's attributions (Lepper, 1983). If parental pressure is pronounced the child may comply, but recognise that the newly adopted behaviour pattern is in response to an *external* control. When this external control is removed, the behaviour will revert. Parents who adopt a more subtle approach, but one that is sufficiently strong to be effective (what the author terms *minimally sufficient*) may produce *internalised* results. The child modifies his behaviour and then rationalises it by attributing it to an internal change.

The Stability of Personality
At the beginning of this chapter brief mention was made of theories which assumed traits of personality which are basic attributes of the

individual, and which are unaffected by variations in the environment. A number of studies have examined the stability of these attributes.

Newman, Freeman, and Holzinger (1937) measured personality variables in identical twins (monozygous twins), some of whom had been raised together and others who had been separated at birth and raised in separate homes. Each pair of twins carries identical genetic make-up, so if personality variables are entirely genetic in origin the home situation should have no effect and all pairs of twins should have identical personalities. (For a full account and appraisal of twin studies see Mittler, 1971). On the other hand, if personality is made up of learned dispositions and behaviours one might expect close similarity for twins reared together but none for twins reared apart. The results were not quite this dramatic, but they did indicate a high degree of similarity for both sets of twins, confirming the influence of genetic factors.

Shields (1962) and Gottesman (1963) came to similar conclusions. In Gottesman's study thirty-four pairs of monozygous and thirty-four pairs of dizygous twins were matched for age, socio-economic status and intelligence, and they were all of the same sex. Using a questionnaire technique the personalities of the children were assessed and compared. Very high degrees of similarity were found between pairs of monozygous twins on such traits as social introversion (the tendency to avoid contact with people) and anxiety, whilst no such relationships were found between dizygous twins.

Twin studies make use of a unique natural phenomenon, the existence of pairs of individuals with similar or identical genetic constitutions. Evidence can be sought elsewhere however, using longitudinal data. Kagan and Moss (1962) assessed the consistency of passivity, aggression and achievement striving from infancy to adulthood. The authors reported that passivity was clearly identifiable by the second year of life and remained relatively constant throughout childhood. The level of aggression in boys was also relatively consistent, as was dependency in girls, but striving for achievement was not discernible until some time in middle childhood. This suggests that it is a learned behaviour, and as such the finding is entirely compatible with the views expressed in the previous section on achievement motivation.

In summary, it would appear that many personality traits do have a fairly strong inherited component. This does not mean that environment is irrelevant, but simply that the range of possible behaviours within a given specified environment will be different for different children. For example, if we imagine a very crude model in which homes which are exceedingly restrictive and authoritarian facilitate aggressive behaviour, and those which are democratic and encourage exploratory activity nurture non-aggressive behaviour, the possible outcome in terms of the aggressive behaviours of any child will depend upon an interaction of inherited trait and home environment (Figure 6.5). It can be seen that there are certain circumstances in which a child with a lower inherited predisposition to agression might actually manifest more agressive behaviour (rated on a scale 1–10) than one who has greater potential for aggression but lives in a more democratically run home. This would be a very simple interaction, and in all probability they are more complex. In Mittler's words 'we understand very little of the nature or quality of the interactions'.

	aggressive trait		
	low	medium	high
authoritarian	5	7	10
average	3	6	7
democratic	1	3	5

Figure 6.4 Hypothetical interaction of inheritance and environment in ratings of aggressive behaviours

Maternal Deprivation

The influence of the home has continually been stressed, and in the early years of childhood it is likely that the mother plays the most influential role in the home, so it is natural that psychologists are interested in what happens to a child if this domestic situation is upset by the absence of the mother figure. Note that we are interested in the absence of the mother figure, that is, the person who takes care of the child. That person could be male or female, and there is no reason to suppose that, from the child's standpoint, the existence of a blood-tie is of any significance. This may not always be true for the caretaker however. A learned belief that there is a special relationship between an infant and its biological parent may help to induce solicitous behaviour and maintain it in very difficult domestic situations.

In 1951 Bowlby published a monograph under the auspices of the World Health Organisation which emphasised that infants must be brought up in a warm, intimate and continuous relationship with the mother figure if mental health was not to be impaired. Whilst Bowlby was not recommending that the caretaker should never be absent, he was, and is, convinced that the child needs to attach to one figure. Part of his evidence came from early studies into the effects of institutional-isation. Many such studies (Goldfarb, 1945; Spitz, 1945) had assessed the effects of child-rearing institutions in which no single person took on the mother's role, as retarding speech and intellectual development, producing acute withdrawal sometimes even to the point of death, and causing maldjusted personalities. Some studies suggested more drastic effects than others, and clearly some institutions may be more impersonal than others, but the views expressed were frequently similar in tone.

These findings were not without criticism however. The forms of deprivation reported in some studies were different from those in others. Some studies did not even describe the form the deprivation took. In many cases it was not possible to determine the levels of adjustment and intellectual functioning in the parents and so the possibility of inherited defects could not be ruled out. Consequently more recent studies have been cautious in their conclusions, and clearer analyses of the forms deprivation has taken have shown that the phenomenon is made up of a number of interrelated features.

This detailed analysis is well represented by the work of Rutter (1981). Whilst acknowledging that genetic and organic factors are also involved, he considers the specific forms of deprivation and their consequences. After taking into account other possibile causes, and the possibilities of inadequately controlled investigations, he nevertheless concludes that many children who are admitted to hospital or residential nursery immediately show acute distress. If these institutions are of 'poor quality' (i.e. lack of stimulation and impersonal treatment) a long stay may result in intellectual impairment, and that 'affectionless psychopathy' (that is, severe emotion impairment involving a failure to respond to, or to give, affection) may follow multiple separation experiences. These general conclusions are amplified by the specification of the forms deprivation may take and some possible links with specific environmental conditions. Acute distress may be caused by severance of the bond with the caretaker, developmental retardation and intellectual impairment by inadequate perceptual and linguistic stimulation, dwarfism by inadequate nutrition, delinquency by family discord, and psychopathy by failure to form attachments in the early years of life. Not only are these physical and psychological mechanisms distinct in character they are also related to the age at which deprivation occurs.

Whilst the term 'maternal deprivation' has often been used to refer to some, or all, of these manifestations, Rutter points out that this is a misnomer. Many of the damaging factors are not specifically tied to the mother, nor do they always involve deprivation. More often the cause is a distortion or lack of relationships, rather than the loss of one already established.

A perplexing feature of 'maternal deprivation' is that some children seem to suffer severe damage, whilst others emerge from similar situations relatively unscathed. Evidence is now suggesting (Graham and George, 1972) that children's temperaments equip them with different degrees of resilience to stressful situations. This may be an inborn characteristic although in many cases the quality of relationships before deprivation may be of considerable importance. In all probability it will depend, once again, upon an interaction of the two.

References

ANNETT, M. (1959) The classification of instances of four common class concepts. *British Journal of Educational Psychology. 29*, 223–36.

ARIES, P. (1973) *Centuries of Childhood*. Harmondsworth, Penguin.

ATKINSON, J. W. (1964) *An Introduction to Motivation*. Princeton, Van Nostrand.

ATKINSON, R. C. & SHIFFRIN, R. M. (1971) The control of short-term memory. *Scientific American*, August 1971, 82–90.

AUSUBEL, D. P. & SULLIVAN, E. V. (Eds.) (1970) *Theory and Problems of Child Development*. New York, Grune & Stratton.

BANDURA, A. (1962) Social learning through imitation. In JONES, M. R. (Ed.) (1962) *Nebraska Symposium on Motivation Vol. 10*. Lincoln, University of Nebraska Press.

BANDURA, A. (1964) The stormy decade: fact or fiction? *Psychology in the Schools. 1*, 224–31.

BANDURA, A., ROSS, D. & ROSS, S. A. (1963a) A comparative test of status envy, social power, and secondary reinforcement theories of identification learning. *Journal of Abnormal and Social Psychology 67*, 527–34.

BANDURA, A., ROSS, D. & ROSS, S. A. (1963b). Vicarious reinforcement and imitative learning. *Journal of Abnormal and Social Psychology. 67*, 601–7.

BERNSTEIN, B. (1960) Language and social class. *British Journal of Sociology. 11*, 271–6.

BERNSTEIN, B. (1971) *Class, codes and control. Vol. 1*. London, Routledge & Kegan Paul.

BLANK, M. (1968) Experimental approaches to concept development in young children. In LUNZER, E. A. & MORRIS, J. F. (1968) *Development in Human Learning*. London, Staples.

BLANK, M. (1975) Commentary in TIZARD, B. (1975) *Early childhood*

Education. Windsor, N. F. E. R.

BLOS, P. (1962) *On Adolescence*. New York, Free Press.

BOWER, T. G. R. (1974) *Development in Infancy*. San Francisco, Freeman.

BRAINE, M. D. S. (1963) The ontogeny of English phrase structure: The first phase. *Language, 39*, 1–13.

BRONFENBRENNER, U. (1960) Freudian theories of identification and their derivatives. *Child Development. 31*, 15–40.

BRONFENBRENNER, U. (1972) *Two Worlds of Childhood*. London, Allen & Unwin.

BROWN, G. (1981) *The place of language in Piagetian Theory*. E. R. I. C. microfilm no. ED 207 055.

BROWN, G. (1983) Metacognition: new insights into old problems? *Brit. J. Educational Studies, 32*, 213–219

BROWN, G & DESFORGES, C. (1979) *Piaget's theory: a psychological critique*. London: R. K. P.

BROWN, G., SHAW, M. & TAYLOR, S. (1969) An experiment to examine the use of four common class concepts by primary school children. *Papers in Education, 1*, 9–11.

BROWN, G., CHERRINGTON, D. H. & COHEN, L. (1975) *Experiments in the Social Sciences*, London, Harper & Row.

BROWN, J. A. C. (1961) *Freud and the Post-Freudians*. Harmondsworth, Penguin.

BROWN, R. (1958) How shall a thing be called? *Psychological Review, 65*, 14–21.

BROWN, R. (1973) *A First Language: the Early Stages*. London, George Allen & Unwin.

BROWN, R. & BELLUGI, U. (1964) Three processes in the child's acquisition of syntax. *Harvard Educational Review, 34*, 133–51

BROWN, R., CAZDEN, C & BELLUGI, U. (1969). The child's grammar from I to III. In HILL, J. P. (Ed.) (1969) *Minnesota Symposium on Child Psychology, Vol. II*. Minneapolis, Minnesota Press.

BROWN, R. & FRASER, C. (1963) The acquisition of syntax. In COFER, C. N. & MUSGRAVE, B. S. (Eds.) (1963) *Verbal Behaviour and Learning: Problems and Processes*. New York, McGraw-Hill.

BROWN, R. & LENNEBERG, E. H. (1954) A study in language and cognition. *Journal of Abnormal and Social Psychology. 49*, 454–62.

BRUNER, J. S. (1964) The course of cognitive growth. *American Psychologist. 19*, 1–15.

BRUNER, J. S. (1975) Language as an instrument of thought. In DAVIES,

A. (Ed.) (1975) *Problems of Language and Learning.* London, Heinemann.

BRUNER, J. S., GOODNOW, J. J. & AUSTIN, G. A. (1956) *A Study of Thinking.* New York, Wiley.

BRUNER, J. S., OLVER, R. R. & GREENFIELD, P. M. (1966) *Studies in Cognitive Growth.* New York, Wiley.

BRUNTLAND, G. H. & WALLØE, E. (1973) Menarcheal age in Norway. *Nature. 241*, 478–9.

BRYANT, P. (1971) Cognitive development. *British Medical Bulletin. 27*, 200–5.

BRYANT, P. (1974) *Perception and Understanding in Young Children.* London, Methuen.

BULL, N. J. (1969) *Moral Judgement from Childhood to Adolescence.* London, Routledge & Kegan Paul.

CARROLL, J. B. (1963) Linguistic relativity, contrastive linguistics, and language learning. *International Review of Applied Linguistics in Language Teaching. I*, 1–20.

CARROLL, J. B. & CASAGRANDE, J. B. (1958). The function of language classifications in behaviour. In MACCOBY, E. E., NEWCOMB, T. M. & HARTLEY, E. L. (Eds.) *Readings in Social Psychology.* London, Methuen.

CATTELL, R. B. (1965) *The Scientific Analysis of Personality.* Harmondsworth, Penguin.

CAZDEN, C. (1965) Environmental assistance to the child's acquisition of grammar. Unpublished doctoral dissertation. Harvard University. Cited in DALE, P. S. (1972) *Language Development.* Illinois, Dryden.

CHARLESWORTH, W. R. & HARTUP, W. W. (1967) Positive social reinforcement in the nursery school peer group. *Child Development. 38*, 993–1002.

CHASE, W. G. & CHI, M. T. H. (1980) Cognitive skills: implications for spatial skill in large-scale environments. In HARVEY, J. (Ed) *Cognition, social behaviour, and the environment.* Potomac: Erlbaum

CHOMSKY, C. S. (1969) *The Acquisition of Syntax in Children from 5 to 10.* Massachusetts, M. I. T. Press.

CHOMSKY, N. (1975) *Syntactic Structures.* The Hague, Mouton.

CHOMSKY, N. (1959) Review of B. F. Skinner's 'Verbal Behavior'. *Language. 35*, 26–58.

CHOMSKY, N. (1965) *Aspects of the Theory of Syntax.* Massachusetts, M. I. T. Press.

CRANDALL, V. J., PRESTON, A. & RABSON, A. (1960) Maternal reactions to the development of independence and achievement behavior in young children. *Child Development. 31,* 243–51.

DALE, P. S. (1972) *Language Development.* Illinois, Dryden.

DANN, T. C. & ROBERTS, D. F. (1973) End of the trend? A 12-year study of age at menarche. *British Medical Journal, 3,* 265–7.

DEESE, J. & KAUFMAN, R. A. (1957) Serial effects in recall of unorganised and sequentially organised verbal material. *J. Experimental Psychology,* 54, 180–187

DENNIS, W. (1940) *The Hopi Child.* New York, Appleton.

DOLLARD, J. & MILLER, N. E. (1950) *Personality and Psychotherapy.* New York, McGraw Hill.

DONALDSON, M. (1978) *Children' minds.* London: Croom Helm

ELDER, G. H. (1968) Adolescent socialization and development. In BORGATTA, E. & LAMBERT, W. (Eds.) (1968). *Handbook of Personality Theory and Research.* Chicago, Rand McNally.

ERIKSON, E. H. (1950) *Childhood and Society.* New York, Norton.

ESCALONA, S. K. (1969) Patterns of infantile experience and the developmental process. *Psychoanalytic Study of Children. 18,* 197–244.

EYSENCK, H. J. (1970) *The Structure of Human Personality.* London, Methuen.

EYSENCK, H. J. (1971) *Race, Intelligence and Education.* London, Temple Smith.

EYSENCK, H. J. versus KAMIN, L. J. (1981) *Intelligence: battle for the mind.* London: Pan

EYSENCK, H. J. & WILSON, G. (1973) *The Experimental Study of Freudian Theories.* London, Methuen.

FANTZ, R. L. (1961) The origin of form perception. *Scientific American. 204,* 66–72.

FANTZ, R. L. (1963) Pattern vision in new-born infants. *Science. 146,* 668–70.

FANTZ, R. L., ORDY, J. M. & UDELF M. A. (1962) Motivation of pattern vision in infants during the first six months. *Journal of Comparative Physiological Psychology. 65,* 907–17.

FEATHERMAN, D. L. (1972) Achievement Orientations and Socio-economic Career Attainments. *American Sociological Review. 37,* 131–43.

FLAVELL, J. H. (1963) *The Developmental Psychology of Jean Piaget.* New York, Van Nostrand.

FLAVELL, J. H. (1971) Commentary in GREEN, D. R., FORD, M. P. & FLAMER, G. B. (Eds.) (1971) *Measurement and Piaget.* New York,

McGraw Hill.

FLAVELL, J. H. (1975) Stage-related properties of cognitive development in MUSSEN, P. H., CONGER, J. J. & KAGAN, J. (Eds.) (1975) *Basic and Comtemporary Issues in Developmental Psychology. 3rd Edn.* New York, Harper and Row.

FODOR, J. (1972) Some reflections on L. S. Vygotsky's 'Thought and Language'. *Cognition. 1*, 83–95.

FRANCIS, H. (1974) Social background, speech and learning to read. *British Journal of Educational Psychology. 44*, 290–9.

FRANCIS, H. (1975) *Language in Childhood*. London, Paul Elek.

FURTH, H. G. (1961) The influence of language in the development of concept formation in deaf children. *Journal of Abnormal and Social Psychology. 63* 386–9.

GARDNER, R. A. & GARDNER, B. T. (1971) Two-way communication with an infant chimpanzee. In SCHRIER, A. M. & STOLLNITZ, F. (Eds.) (1971) *Behaviour of Non-human Primates, Vol. 4.* New York, Academic Press.

GESELL, A., THOMPSON, H. & AMATRUDA, C. S. (1934) *Infant Behaviour: its Genesis and Growth.* New York, McGraw-Hill.

GIBSON, E. J., GIBSON, J. J., PICK, A. D. & OSSER, H. (1962) A developmental study of the discrimination of letter-like forms. *Journal of Comparative Physiological Psychology. 55*, 897–906.

GOLDFARB, W. (1945) Psychological privation in infancy and subsequent adjustment. *American Journal of Orthopsychiatry. 15*, 247–55.

GOTTESMAN, I. I. (1963) Genetic aspects of intelligent behaviour. In ELLIS, N. R. (ed.) (1963) *Handbook of Mental Deficiency.* New York, McGraw Hill.

GRAHAM, D. (1972) *Moral Learning and Development.* London, Batsford.

GRAHAM, P. & GEORGE, S. (1972) Children's response to parental illness: individual differences. Cited by RUTTER, M. (1972) *Maternal Deprivation Reassessed.* Harmondsworth, Penguin.

GRANT, N. (1964) *Soviet Education.* Harmondsworth, Penguin.

GREENE, J. (1972) *Psycholinguistics.* Harmondsworth, Penguin.

GULIFORD, R. (1971) *Special Educational Needs.* London, Routledge & Kegan Paul.

GUSTIN, J. C. (1961) The revolt of youth. *Psychoanalysis and the Psychoanalytic Review. 98*, 78–90.

HALL, G. S. (1904) *Adolescence.* New York, Appleton.

HEIDER, F. (1958) *The psychology of interpersonal relations.* N. York: Wiley.

HELD, R. & HEIN, A. (1963) Movement produced stimulation in the development of visually guided behaviour. *Journal of Comparative Physiological Psychology. 56*, 872–6.

HESS, R. D. & SHIPMAN, V. C. (1965) Early experience and the socialization of cognitive modes in children. *Child Development, 36* 860–6.

H. M. S. O. (1931) *The Primary School.* Report of Consultative Committee of Council.

HUBEL, D. H. & WIESEL, T. N. (1963) Receptive fields of cells in striate cortex of very young, visually inexperienced kittens. *Journal of Neurophysiology. 26*, 994–1002.

HUTTENLOCHER, J. (1974) The origins of language comprehension. In SOLSO, R. L. (ed.) (1974) *Theories in Cognitive Psychology.* Loyola, University of Chicago.

ILLINGWORTH, R. S. (1966) *The Development of the Infant and Young Child, 3rd Ed.* Edinburgh and London, Livingstone.

INHELDER, B. & SINCLAIR, H. (1969) Learning cognitive structures. In MUSSEN, P. H., LANGER, J. & COVINGTON, M. (1969) *Trends and Issues in Developmental Psychology.* New York, Holt, Rinehart & Winston.

JAMES, W. (1980) *Principles of Psychology.* New York, Holt.

JENSEN, A. R. (1969) *Environment, Heredity and Intelligence.* Harvard Reprint Series No. 2.

JONES, M. C. (1924) Elimination of children's fears. *Journal of Experimental Psychology. 7*, 382–90.

KAGAN, J. (1969) *Personality Development.* New York, Harcourt, Brace, Jovanovich.

KAGAN, J. & MOSS, J. (1962) *From Birth To Maturity* New York, Wiley.

KAHL, J. A. (1953) Common man boys. In HALSEY, A. H., FLOUD, J. & ANDERSON, C. A. (eds.) (1961) *Education, Economy and Society.* Glencoe, Illinois, Free Press.

KAIL, R. (1984) *The development of memory in children: 2nd. Edn.* N. York: Freeman.

KAMIN, L. J. (1974) *The science and politics of I.Q.* Potomac: Erlbaum

KATKOVSKY., PRESTON, A. & CRANDALL, V. J. (1964 a) Parental attitudes toward their personal achievements and toward the achievement behaviours of their children. *Journal of Genetic Psychology. 104*, 67–82.

KATKOVSKY, W., PRESTON, A. & CRANDALL, V. J. (1964 b) Parents' achievement attitudes and their behaviour with their children in achievement situations. *Journal of Genetic Psychology. 104*, 105–21.

KAYE, K. (1984) *The mental and social life of babies.* London: Methuen.

KELLY, M. & PHILIP, H. (1975) Vernacular test instructions in relation to cognitive task behaviour among highland children of Papua New Guinea. *British Journal of Educational Psychology*. *45*. 189–97.

KENDLER, H. H. & KENDLER, T. S. (1961) Effects of verbalization on reversal shifts in children. *Science*. *134*, 1619–20.

KLEIN, M. (1932) *Psycho-analysis of Children*. London, Hogarth.

KLINE, P. (1981) *Fact and Fantasy in Freudian Theory; 2nd Edn*. London, Methuen.

KOHLBERG, L. (1963) The development of children's orientations toward a moral order. *Vita Humana*. *6*, 11–33.

KOHLBERG, L. (1964) The development of moral character. In HOFFMAN, M. L. & HOFFMAN, L. W. (eds.) (1964) *Review of Child Development Research, Vol. I*. New York, Russell Sage.

LABOV, W. (1969) The logic of nonstand English. *Georgetown Monographs on Language and Linguistics*. *22*. 1–22; 26–31.

LAWTON, D. (1968) *Social Class, Language, and Education*. London, Routledge & Kegan Paul.

LEPPER, M. (1983) Social control processes and the internalization of social values: an attributional perspective. In HIGGINS, E. T., RUBLE, D. & HATRUP, W. (eds) *Social cognition and social development: a socio-cultural perspective*. N. York: Cambridge U. P.

LEWIN, K. (1952) Time perspective and morale. In WATSON, G. (ed.) (1952) *Civilian Morale*. New York, Houghton Mifflin.

LEWIS, M. M. (1951) *Infant Speech, 2nd ed*. London, Routledge & Kegan Paul.

LEWIS, M. & GOLDBERG, S. (1969) The acquisition and violation of expectancy: an experimental paradigm. *Journal of Experimental Child Psychology*. *7*, 70–80.

LOVELL, K. (1964) *The Growth of Basic Mathematical and Scientific Concepts in Children, 3rd ed*. London, University of London Press.

LOVELL, K. (1968) *An Introduction to Human Development*. London, Macmillan.

LUNZER, E. A. (1960) Recent Studies in Britain based on the work of Jean Piaget. *Occasional Publications No. 4*. London, N.F.E.R.

LUNZER, E. A. (1968) *The Regulation of Behaviour*. London, Staples.

LURIA, A. R. & YUDOVITCH, F. (1959) *Speech and the Development of Mental Processes in the Child*. London, Staples.

LYONS, J. (1970) *Chomsky*. London, Fontana.

MACCOBY, E. E. (1959) Role taking in childhood and its consequences for social learning. *Child Development*. *30*, 239–52.

MCCLELLAND, D. C. (1958) The use of measures of human motivation in the study of society. In ATKINSON, J. W. (ed.) *Motives in Fantasy, Action, and Society*. Princeton, Van Nostrand.

MCCLELLAND, D. C., ATKINSON, S., CLARK, R. & LOWELL. E. (1953) *The Achievement Motive*. New York, Appleton Century Crofts.

MCNEILL, D. (1970) *The Acquisition of Language*. New York, Harper & Row.

MCNEILL, D. (1973) Sentence structure in chimpanzee communication. In CONNOLLY, K. J. & BRUNER, J. S. (eds.) (1973) *The Growth of Competence*. London, Academic Press.

MALINOWSKI, B. (1927) *Sex and Repression in Savage Society*. New York, Harcourt Brace.

MEAD, M. (1962) *Male and Female*. Harmondsworth, Penguin.

MELZACK, R. (1965) Effects of early experience of behaviour: experimental and conceptual considerations. In HOCH, P. H. & ZUBIN, J. (eds.) *Psychopathology of Perception*. New York, Grune and Stratton.

MILLER, G. A. (1962) Some psychological studies of grammar. *American Psychologist. 17*, 748–62.

MISCHEL, W. (1976) *Introduction to personality: 2nd. Edn.* N. York: Holt, Rinehart & Winston.

MITTLER, P. (1971) *The Study of Twins*. Harmondsworth, Penguin.

MORRIS, J. F. (1958) The development of adolescent value judgements. *British Journal of Educational Psychology. 28*, 97–102.

MOWRER, O. H. (1960) *Learning Theory and the Symbolic Processes*. New York, Wiley.

MUSSEN, P. H., CONGER, J. J. & KAGAN, J. (1963) *Child Development and Personality*. New York, Harper & Row.

NASH, J. (1970) *Developmental Psychology: A Psychobiological Approach*. New Jersey, Prentice-Hall.

NEISSER, U. (1967) *Cognitive Psychology*. New York, Appleton-Century-Crofts.

NEISSER, U. & WEENE, P. (1960) A note on human recognition of hand-printed characters. *Information and Control. 3*, 191–6.

NEWMAN, H. H., FREEMAN, F. N. & HOLZINGER, K. J. (1937) *Twins: A study of Heredity and Environment*. Chicago, University of Chicago Press.

NEWSON, J. & NEWSON, E. (1970) *Patterns of Infant Care*. Harmondsworth, Penguin.

OLERON, P. (1953) Conceptual thinking of the deaf. *American Annals of the Deaf. 98*, 304–10.

OLSON, D. R. (1966) On conceptual strategies. In BRUNER, J. S., OLVER, R. R. & GREENFIELD, P. M. (1966) *Studies in Cognitive Growth*. New York, Wiley.

PARTEN, M. L. (1932) Social participation among preschool children. *Journal of Abnormal and Social Psychology. 27*, 243–69.

PIAGET, J. (1932) *The Moral Judgement of the Child*. London, Routledge & Kegan Paul.

PIAGET, J. (1950) *The Psychology of Intelligence*. London, Routledge & Kegan Paul.

PIAGET, J. (1954) *The Construction of Reality in the Child*. New York, Basic Books.

PIAGET, J. (1972) Intellectual evolution from adolescence to adulthood. *Human Development. 15*, 1–12.

PIAGET, J. & INHELDER, B. (1969) *The Psychology of the Child*. London, Routledge & Kegan Paul.

POPPER, K. R. (1974) *Conjectures and Refutations, 5th ed*. London, Butler & Tanner.

RICHARDSON, K. & SPEARS, D. (eds.) (1972) *Race, Culture and Intelligence*. Harmondsworth, Penguin.

RICKS, D. M. (1972) The beginnings of vocal communication in infants and autistic children. Unpublished M. D. thesis, University of London. Cited by CROMER, R. F. (1974) The development of language and cognition: the Cognition Hypothesis. In Foss, B. (1974) *New Perspectives in Child Development*. Harmondsworth, Penguin.

ROBINSON, E. J. & ROBINSON, W. P. (1982) The advancement of children's referential communication skills: the role of metacognitive guidance. *J. International Behaviour Development*. 5,329–55.

ROSEN, B. C. & D'ANDRADE, R. (1959) The Psychosocial Origins of Achievement Motivation. *Sociometry. 22*, 185–218.

ROSEN, H. (1972) *Language and Class*. Bristol, Falling Wall Press.

ROSENBAUM, R. M. (1972) A dimensional analysis of the perceived causes of success and failure. Unpublished Ph.D. thesis, University of California. cited by WEINER, B. (1974) *Achievement motivation and attribution theory*. Morristown, N. J.: General Learning Press.

ROTTER, J. B. (1966) Generalized expectancies for internal versus external control of reinforcement. *Psychological Monographs. 80*, 1–28 (no. 609)

RUTTER, M. (1981) *Maternal Deprivation Reassessed: 2nd Edn*. Harmondsworth, Penguin.

RYAN, J. (1974) Early language development: towards a communicational analysis. In RICHARDS, M. P. M. (1974) *The Integration of a Child into a Social World*. Cambridge, Cambridge University Press.

SCAMMON, R. E. (1930) In HARRIS, J. A. *et al* (1930) *The Measurement of Man*. Minneapolis, University of Minnesota Press.

SCARDAMALIA, M. (1981) How children cope with the cognitive demands of writing. In FREDERIKSEN, C. H. & DOMINIC, J. F. (eds) *Writing; the nature, development and teaching of written communication*. Hillsdale, N. J.: Erlbaum.

SCHAFFER, H. R. (1971) *The Growth of Sociability*. Harmondsworth, Penguin.

SEARS, R. R., MACCOBY, E. E. & LEVIN, H. (1957) *Patterns of Child-Rearing*. New York, Row Peterson.

SEARS, R. R., RAU, L. & ALPERT, R. (1965) *Identification and Child Rearing*. Stanford, Stanford University Press.

SHEINFELD, A. (1973) *Twins and Supertwins*. Harmondsworth, Penguin.

SHERIDAN, M. D. (1973) *Children's Developmental Progress from Birth to Five Years: The Stycar Sequences*. Slough, N.F.E.R.

SHIELDS, J. (1962) *Monozygotic Twins Brought Up Together and Apart*. Oxford, Oxford University Press.

SKINNER, B. F. (1953) *Science and Human Behaviour*. New York, Macmillan.

SKINNER, B. F. (1957) *Verbal Behaviour*. New York, Appleton-Century-Crofts.

SLOBIN, D. I. (1971) *Psycholinguistics*. Illinois, Scott Foresman.

SMEDSLUND, J. (1961) The acquisition of the conservation of substance and weight in children. *Scandinavian Journal of Psychology*. 2, 85–92, 153–5, 155–60, 203–10.

SMITH, C. P. (ed.) (1969) *Achievement – Related Motives in Children*. New York, Russell Sage.

SITH, F. (1973) *Psycholinguistics and Reading*. New York, Holt.

SMITH, M. C. (1978) Cognizing the behaviour stream: the recognition of intentional acts. *Child Development*. 49, 736–43.

SMITH, P. K., CONNOLLY, K. & FLEMING, D. (1972) Environment and behaviour in a playgroup: effects of varying physical resources. *Man-Environment Systems, 2*, 254–6.

SPERLING, G. (1960) The information available in brief visual presentations. *Psychological Monographs*. 74 (whole of 498)

SPITZ, R. A. (1945) Hospitalism: an enquiry into the genesis of psychiatric conditions in early childhood. *Psychoanalytic Studies of Children.* 2, 53–74.

TANNER, J. M. (1961) *Education and Physical Growth.* London, University of London Press.

TANNER, J. M. (1962) *Growth at Adolescence.* London, Blackwell.

TANNER, J. M. (1978) *Foetus into man.* London, Open Books.

TARANGER, J. (1983) Secular changes in sexual maturation. *Acta Medica Auxologica.* 15, 137–50.

TIZARD, B. (1974) *Early Childhood Education.* Windsor, N.F.E.R.

TREVARTHEN, C. (1975) Early attempts at speech. In LEWIN, C. (ed) *Child alive.* London: Temple Smith.

TURNER, R. H. (1969) Role-taking: process versus conformity. In LINDESMITH, A. R. & STRAUS, A. L. (eds.) (1969) *Readings in Social Psychology.* New York, Holt, Rinehart & Winston.

VON SENDEN, M. (1932) *Space and Sight.* (trans. by P. Heath) New York, Free Press.

VYGOTSKY, L. S. (1962) *Thought and Language.* New York, Wiley.

WATSON, J. B. & RAYNOR, R. (1920) conditional emotional reactions. *Journal of Experimental Psychology.* 3, 1–14.

WATSON, J. D. & CRICK, F. H. C. (1953) Molecular structure of nucleic acids. *Nature.* 171, 173–8.

WEINER, B. (1980) *Human motivation.* N. York: Holt, Rinehart & Winston

WELLMAN, H. M. (1977) Tip of the tongue and feeling of knowing experiences: a developmental study of memory-monitoring. *Child Development.* 48, 13–21.

WILKINSON, A. (1985) Writing. In BENNETT, S. N. & DESFORGES, C. (eds) *Recent advances in classroom research.* Brit. J. Educ. Psychology Monograph Series No 2.

WINTERBOTTOM, M. R. (1958) The relationship of need for achievement to learning experiences in independence and mastery. In ATKINSON, J. W. (ed.) (1958) *Motives in Fantasy, Action & Society.* Princeton, Van Nostrand.

WOHLWILL, J. F. (1968) Amount of stimulus exploration and preference as differential functions of stimulus. *Perception and Psychophysics,* 3, 439–44.

WOLFF, J. L. (1967) Concept-shift and discrimination-reversal learning in humans. *Psychological Bulletin.* 68, 369–403.

WOLFF, P. H. (1969) The national history of crying and other vocalizations in early infancy. In FOSS, B. M. (ed.) (1969) *Determinants of Infant Behaviour, IV.* London, Methuen.

Subject Index

adaptation 71
accommodation 69–71, 106
adolescence 34–6, 76, 122–3
anal fixation 115
anxiety 119, 128
assimilation 69–71, 106
attention 47–8
attributions 134–5

Burt, Cyril 1

cataracts 46
cephalocaudal principle 28–9
chromosome 19–28
concepts 53–86
   hierachy 58–9
conceptual strategy 64–9
constituent analysis 102
contentive words 93
crying 88

deep structure 104
developmental age 31–3
Dewey, John 2
discrimination learning 118
Down's syndrome 26
drives 118

echoic response 99–100
echoing 94
egocentrism 72, 110
equilibration 71
expressivity 25
eye colour 23, 24

fear 120–1
fixation 113
functional invariants 70–1
functors 93

gamete, germ cell 19
generalisation 118
generative linguistics 103–6
genetic epistemology 69

genetic structure 19–28
genotype 25
gestalt 41
grasping 37–8

habituation 47
haemolytic incompatibility 27
holophrase 89–90
Hopi Indian 30, 59
hypothesis 4–5

id, ego, superego 113–15, 128–9
idea scheme 95
identification 115–16, 119–20
intelligence 24
intersubjectivity 110

Language acquisition device (LAD) 105
language, in primates 98
libido 113
linguistic codes 69–70, 108–9
linguistic competence 103
linguistic performance 103
Locke, John 2
locus of control 134

mand 99
Markov process 100–1
maternal deprivation 137–9
Melpa 60
memory 82–6
   primary 83–4, 86
   secondary 84–5
metalanguage 95
metamemory 86
mitosis 19, 20
mnemonics 85
mongolism, Down's syndrome 26
Montessori, M. 2
morality 127–31
morpheme 98
Müller-Lyer illusion 41

Navaho Indian 60

object scheme 95
oedipal situation 115–16, 128
open and pivot words 90–1
oral fixation 115
ossification 33

pendulum experiment 75–6
penetrance 25
penis envy 116, 128
perception, constancy of 42–3
    pattern and form 43–7
Pestalozzi, J.H. 2
phenotype 25
phenylketonurea, PKU 27
phoneme 98
phrase structure grammar 102–3
Plato 1
Pleasure Principle 113
pre-speech 125
primacy effect 84
Principle of Reversibility 73
prompting 94
proximodistal principle 29
puberty 33–6
punishment 130–1

reaction formation 117
Reality Principle 113
recall 83, 84, 85
recency effect 84
recognition 83, 85
reflex 36–7
representation,
    enactive 63
    iconic 63–4
    symbolic 64
research design,
    cross-sectional 8, 9
    longitudinal 7–8, 9
    sampling 7

role 121–3
Rousseau, J.J. 2
rules, 129–30

Sapir-Whorf hypothesis 59–60
second signal system 82
sensory register 83
sex 23–5
socialization 111–27
sound scheme 95
speech 3, 87–97
stages, concept of 15–18
    concrete operations 74–5
    formal operations 75–6
    pre–operations 72–4
    sensori-motor 71–2
structures 70
subliminal stimuli 40
surface structure 104
syntax 105

tact 99
telegraphic speech 92–3
template 49–52
tests
    developmental 11
    intelligence 10
traits 112
transfer and transposition 79–82
transformational grammar 103–6
twins 25–6, 30–1, 99, 136

visual cliff 43, 45
Vygotsky's blocks 60–63

Washoe 98
written language 107–8

Zuni Indian 59
zygote 19, 21, 28